Going Global

Going Global

Culture, Gender, and Authority in the Japanese Subsidiary of an American Corporation

Ellen V. Fuller

 TEMPLE UNIVERSITY PRESS
Philadelphia

Temple University Press
Philadelphia, Pennsylvania 19122
www.temple.edu/tempress

Copyright © 2009 by Temple University
All rights reserved
Published 2009
Printed in the United States of America

♾ The paper used in this publication meets the requirements of the
American National Standard for Information Sciences—Permanence of
Paper for Printed Library Materials, ANSI z39.48-1992

Library of Congress Cataloging-in-Publication Data

Fuller, Ellen V., 1956–
    Going global : culture, gender and authority in the Japanese subsidiary of an
American corporation / Ellen V. Fuller.
        p. cm.
    Includes bibliographical references and index.
    ISBN 978-1-59213-688-9 (cloth : alk. paper) — ISBN 978-1-59213-689-6 (pbk. :
alk. paper)   1. Corporations, American—Japan—Social aspects.   2. International
business enterprises—Japan—Employees.   3. Corporate culture—Japan.
4. Management—Japan.   I. Title.
    HD2907.F85   2008
    331.6'9956—dc22   2008022366

100317P

For Brad;
for Jerry, Keelie, Leo, Max, Oscar, and P;
and for Rachel

Contents

 Preface

This book began as a dissertation, and the dissertation began as part of a quest to expand my horizons in East Asia. I had earned degrees focused on China and had spent considerable time there as well as Hong Kong and Taiwan. En route to those places, I sometimes had opportunities to travel in Japan and my intellectual interest grew. I started learning the language and reading widely before deciding to focus on Japan in a Ph.D. program at Stanford University. My M.B.A. was supposed to be my last stop in higher education, but while pursuing that degree many of the questions that drove the fieldwork for this book first arose.

In addition to a lifelong interest in East Asia, I have been concerned for an equally long time with understanding the dynamics of gender. First and foremost, I operate from the assumption that discrimination today is rarely a conscious intention; rather, it operates in the spaces between, in the interstices of people's interactions with one another. The people of Transco who served as the subjects of this book, including everyone right up to the most senior management, do not expressly seek to raise up certain categories of people at the expense of others. In my day-to-day scrutiny of Transco, I came to feel strongly that meritocracy was the desired outcome.

The problem was that meritocracy did not seem to me to be in the offing; at best, it was coming at a pace so glacial (pre–global warming) that women and Japanese would have to wait decades for opportunities that truly were unfettered by considerations of their gender and culture. This book is in part a cautionary tale for senior management—if you truly want to make full use of the capabilities of all of your employees, including yourselves, you need to consider your own impact on the processes of employee development beyond what may be found in the creation of corporate principles as well as rationalized criteria of advancement in an organization.

Before going to Japan for fieldwork, I had targeted Transco as my research site based on a connection through my university. It turned out that the connection was no longer in place, but fortuitously the new head of Transco, "Walter" in the text that follows, had an ardent interest in fostering the advancement of managerial Japanese females at the company. Thus he responded enthusiastically to my request to conduct fieldwork there, seeing it as a potential opportunity to expand his own knowledge with little or no cost to the organization. We spent considerable time, particularly given his busy schedule, simply talking. Although he was aware that he, too, was a research subject, he openly shared his opinions and enthusiastically engaged in debate. He also provided me with office space on the top floor of the building, connection to the phone and messaging system, and helped me to choose the six primary subjects, based on his assessments of their strengths and weaknesses.

In my research, the top-floor location brought both advantages and disadvantages. On the plus side, the location served to validate further the perceptions of managers on the floors below that I had strong support from senior executives to carry out my research. As a result, I think more managers cooperated with me more readily. In reality, I was surprised by the friendly openness of most people in management. On the minus side, a couple of managers were suspicious of my presence, wondering if I were on some sort of secret mission for the chief executives in Japan. I learned about these people through gossip as I became more accepted as a "grape on the vine." One of these people was the only one who ever turned down a request I made to observe a meeting; I was given the option to "go over his head" but chose not to do so.

Overwhelmingly, I was given access to many more sources of information and opportunities for observation than I anticipated, primarily owing to the generosity of Walter. The note he left on my desk one day aptly sums up my time at the company; in response to yet another request from me for permission to attend such-and-such event, it read: "Ellen, you are welcome anytime, anywhere." It turned out to be a literal statement as I was, in fact, given access to confidential information and allowed even to attend private strategy meetings. It was an expression of trust for which I remain ever mindful and grateful. Transco was both generous and gracious, and any fault with this research lies solely with me.

My location on the top floor also required negotiation with a few of the regular employees. For example, one secretary expressed reluctance to fill out one of my anonymous surveys that were mailed back to me in sealed envelopes via the top floor mailroom because she thought it might be read by the senior Japanese secretaries (but not the American executives, interestingly enough) who also had mail delivered there. Nevertheless, she came to me, told me what prevented her from replying as requested, and agreed to give me her answers in person.

Over time I was able to undo potential problems with my physical location and unclear status by developing a positive reputation simply because of the dictates of the fieldwork. I was very conscious of trying to establish myself as someone who was open, objective, and confidential. I chose "observation of Transco" rather than "participant observation at Transco" to give employees the freedom to choose or refuse to interact with me under the full knowledge of my reasons for being there. If I sacrificed some of the true picture of the place as a result of this decision, I think the sacrifice amounts to very little, at least as might be evidenced by the fact that people fought openly at meetings that I attended and that interviewees sometimes would blanch in the middle of an interview, saying that they could not believe they had just told me something, only to continue.

The globalization campaign that is outlined in the text caused a marked rise in Japanese employees' criticisms of Americans and American culture, particularly on the score of limited ability to understand "the real Japan." It is important to note that when I returned to Transco in 1999 for follow-up research, tensions had cooled down considerably, but people still talked about globalization in the same way they had in 1997, often using identical words and phrases, even though the idea of globalization was more accepted and no longer perceived as such a threat. These repetitive patterns of thought are an indication that cultural tensions at Transco will not be fully resolved without some new approaches to management of employees.

Because I arrived at a time when the globalization drive was causing Japanese employees to be hypercritical of the American management's understanding of Japan, these same employees accorded increased significance to my status as a Japan specialist in ways that augmented my research efforts. I studied Japan as a career and both spoke and read Japanese. I asked questions and listened without offering opposing viewpoints, trying to learn. I knew all sorts of "odd" details about Japan and the Japanese.

Vis-à-vis the expatriated management, then, I came to be regarded, whether correctly or not, as someone who "got it." My status as an American studying Transco with the support of the American management, coupled with my knowledge of and interest in Japan for its own sake, led me to be perceived as a conduit for the potential flow of information from the Japanese to the Americans at Transco. Knowledge of my existence at Transco seemed to spread rapidly through the organization. Thus, not only were many Japanese employees willing to be interviewed and to allow me to follow them around and attend their meetings, but a number of Japanese employees who fell outside the scope of my daily observations requested that I include them in my interviews.

I have chosen to keep the identity of the corporation anonymous even though I was not obligated to do so; my research contract required only that I not reveal any strategic secrets. Walter joked one day that he would like me to use the true corporate name if the outcome of my study were positive, but not if the outcome were negative, to which I responded with my own humor that a perfectly positive assessment of Transco would likely lead to a rather negative assessment of my dissertation.

Despite media and other characterizations of academia as biased toward the liberal, however, this study has nothing to do with that. A major purpose of this inquiry is to identify what might need improvement in the organization so that all categories of people at Transco, including the senior white male management, can operate to the best of their abilities and encourage the same in others without reducing one another to meaningless caricatures based on sweeping generalizations. Meritocracy will not occur otherwise. This is surely true for organizations that operate within one single context; it is all the more true for globalizing corporations like Transco. Comparatively speaking, I think that Transco treats its employees well, but that is precisely one reason why it has the capability to push itself further toward real rather than imagined meritocracy.

Acknowledgments

Many people and organizations deserve thanks for their contributions to my formal and informal education, their support of my endeavors to study in Japan, and their general enthusiasm for both me and my work beyond what I could ever have imagined to deserve. Tom Rohlen served as my doctoral advisor at Stanford University. His grace, intelligence, and sense of humor were instrumental to my education there, and I thoroughly enjoyed the challenges of being his student. Myra Strober and Francisco Ramirez served on my dissertation committee, providing detailed comments on my thesis and, along with Woody Powell, probing questions during a thesis defense that turned out to be an intellectual delight.

At the University of Virginia, Michael Kubovy became my mentor for one year while I was the recipient of a University Teaching Fellowship. We spent many hours discussing interdisciplinary approaches to scholarship. Gary Allinson was both a friend and a supporter; I count his books on the history of Japan among the best that I have read.

I met Jack Huddleston while in an M.B.A. program at the University of Washington, and both in his class and beyond we disagreed on almost everything, but our mutual love of respectful debate turned into a long-term friendship. Both he and Gary are much missed.

I want also to thank the anonymous readers in international business and the sociology of Japan for their extensive and helpful commentaries on the manuscript. Mick Gusinde-Duffy has been a gracious editor at Temple, pushing me along while giving me the room I needed to complete the work.

None of this research would have happened without support from the people of Transco, my subjects for this book. At all levels of the organization, they were generous with their time, open with their opinions, and welcoming day in and day out even though I was no doubt a burden at times. I am lucky to be able to count some of them as friends, and I wish the best for each and every one of them.

Nor would the research have happened without the financial support I received from the Blakemore Foundation, the Stanford Institute for International Studies, the David L. Boren Graduate Fellowship program, the University of Virginia Summer Research Awards and University Teaching Fellowship, and the Ellen Bayard Weedon East Asia Travel Grants.

Among family and friends, I am grateful to many, but have room to name only a few. Brad Reed, my partner, is an unending source of love and support. Charles Fuller, my father, calls regularly just to ask how things are going. Liz Perry first introduced me to Japan. The women in my "dinner group" (Hanadi Al-Samman, Mehr Farooqi, Neeti Nair, and Rina Williams) provide me with many kinds of helpful conversation. I want also to extend a special thanks to Bert and Sue Blikslager, Victoria Blikslager O'Hara, and all the denizens of Wolf Trap Farm in whose company the morning fog is sure to lift.

1 Culture, Gender, and Authority in Transnational Corporate Contexts

This study concerns itself with the men and women who work for the Japanese subsidiary of an American corporation that I call Transco. The pseudonym reflects the parent corporation's move toward a transnational corporate culture rather than a multinational one as part of a new globalization strategy. One idea contained within this strategy is that a transnational corporation, by virtue of its more interconnected structure, can create a relatively seamless, global corporate culture that is readily understood and operant at each geographic point around the world.

Originally I went to Japan in 1996 to research the nature of gender and authority in the cross-cultural workplace; specifically, I wanted to learn how Japanese women fare in an American organization that professes equal treatment of men and women in its hiring and promotion practices, as Transco does. Merit, as measured by objective criteria of evaluation, is the hiring and promotion policy claimed to be in effect throughout the parent corporation worldwide. Transco further claims special attention to the hiring, promotion, and retention of college-educated Japanese women as one competitive advantage in Japan, where Transco's native competitors still tend to hire and promote mostly Japanese men.

However, when I arrived on site in 1997 to begin my observations, many of the Japanese employees I met initially were eager to know whether the organization seemed to me to be "Japanese" or "American" in atmosphere. Having spent the preceding year in another part of Japan studying Japanese, conducting library research, and interviewing Japanese friends and acquaintances who had worked for both Japanese and foreign firms, I had to admit that the place felt very "American" to me. It was curious that one after another, those who asked seemed quite pleased by my response, as if my answer were just the one they wanted to hear.

As I was soon to discover, the question of Transco being Japanese or American in tone was very much on the minds of its Japanese employees at the time, and the senior American management had similar concerns, albeit with opposite conclusions. Although the new campaign of globalization was under way, mandated by Transco's parent organization for all offices world-wide, no mention of this campaign had been made to me when I previously visited Transco to meet with the senior American management and set up my research. To the Americans at Transco, global restructuring was not a source of concern for the successful development of the subsidiary, but its "Japanese-ness" was; to the Japanese, globalization was of great concern because of its potential impact on both the corporate culture of Transco and the importance of Japan as a consumer market.

The globalization campaign heightened the cultural tension at Transco and became one vehicle by which culture could be viewed, but culture was an issue in its own right even before the campaign began. Members of the senior American management told me they thought that Transco was still "too Japanese" to be allowed to run on its own without express direction from expatriated management, while the Japanese employees confided that Transco was "very American," and they doubted the ability of the American management to discern the difference between American culture and global culture. Although no one seemed to have a clear conception of global culture, everyone at Transco thought they knew the American and Japanese cultures quite well.

The Japanese used my answer—that the place felt American to me—as proof that they were right. Unlike the expatriated management, I was an American who both studied and lived in the "real" Japan. Hence my opinion was used to counter directly that of the other Americans. I soon realized that the Japanese had vested me with a kind of cultural authority over this topic because of their perception of my dual status: culturally, I was placed somewhere in between the Japanese employees and the expatriated managers and was expected to understand clearly the Japanese vantage point. The globalization drive outlined later in this chapter became one tool for my assessment of cultural strain at Transco because Japanese employees were so concerned with its potentially negative effects. At one point, someone told me that I served as "a well, into which people could shout their anxieties" at this time of upheaval.

Besides enabling new levels to my research, this act on the part of the Japanese employees to position me, as the outside observer, into a dual status in terms of cultural understanding also reflects a power imbalance at Transco. For their part, the American managers did not attempt the same thing. They had no perceived need for me to understand their side of things because they held most of the power, but it was also true that most of the expatriated management assumed I agreed with them on various and sundry issues simply because I was American. They took my positions for granted, if they thought about them at all.

Thus I was made party to all sorts of blanket statements about the Japanese versus American peoples and the cultural superiority of the American way of doing things, at least insofar as management at Transco was concerned. The Japanese also engaged in a great variety of stereotypic comparisons, but theirs was the perspective "from below" as set against the Americans' view "from above." These perspectives were both literal and figurative: the former in terms of relative placement in the organizational hierarchy, in which the Americans were mostly senior managers and the Japanese were mostly subordinate employees, and the latter in terms of perceived differences in power to define the culture of Transco.

Culture appeared to be one dominant framework for employee interactions with one another at Transco, but that framework consisted of mixed types of cultural assessments that regularly moved in opposing directions. There was the presumption of greater cultural similarities when employees of a single nationality met together for some work-related goal and the presumption of greater cultural differences when employees of multiple nationalities were working together, but people did not necessarily agree on the precise nature of those similarities and differences. Individual attitudes about the respective values of the Japanese and American cultures often conflicted with one another. And gender differences in attitudes toward national cultures and the culture of Transco set Japanese women apart from Japanese men.

The differences (and similarities) between the Japanese and the Americans in their attitudes toward culture had many ramifications, with subsequent impacts on gender and authority as well as the culture of Transco itself. Every interaction at Transco seemed to be under the weight of constant negotiation, but in the meantime employees had still to decide how to behave at work, and their individual perceptions of culture, gender, and authority all intertwined to affect this decision making.

Culture is an elusive and often misused concept. Much of what was assumed to be the result of culture at Transco could have been considered instead as behavioral and personality characteristics that transcend culture, but employees of all nationalities and at all levels were heavily invested in culture's relevance to the organization. During my fieldwork, then, I looked at gender and authority at Transco particularly within the parameters of the parent corporation's strategic move toward a globalized corporate culture, and I observed that *culture* and *gender* shared many types of (mis)applications. People throughout the organization relied on their interpretations of these concepts to make decisions about individual and groups of employees, about the nations of Japan and the United States, and about Transco as a place to work and manage. My primary goal in writing this book is to offer parallel presentations and analyses of culture and gender, with the attendant effects on both assumption of authority and organizational effectiveness at Transco.

Another goal is to approach my analyses from both an interdisciplinary and a practical perspective. The following questions drove the fieldwork:

Is it necessary to become like an American to be successful on the job? What does it mean to do so? Or is it enough just to know how to interact effectively with Americans?

How responsible are the Americans for learning to interact with the Japanese?

Who are the Japanese who get promoted, and why do some not make it as far as they would like to go?

Do Japanese women want to be promoted to the highest levels of the organization? If so, do they have an equal chance at promotion? Do they have to subscribe to certain female stereotypes to increase their chances?

Does the corporation see itself in Japan as American or Japanese or global, and what are the differences?

What does the corporation understand to be, and respect as, the unique qualities of both Japan and the Japanese, or do those kinds of evaluations become moot in a global corporation?

These questions are not easy to answer if one sticks to a singular point of view. Therefore, I will take advantage of several decades of scholarship in both the social sciences and the humanities,[1] as well as consider issues of practicality, in seeking answers to these questions.

It is necessary to point out that my fieldwork at Transco represents but one segment of time, the late 1990s. I do not propose to analyze the company overall; rather, my goal is to evaluate the struggles that took place within that time frame over the following issues: globalization; gender; and American and Japanese assessments of one another, as each person sought a comfortable place within a seeming myriad of organizational change. These are struggles that any corporation potentially faces as it moves strategically from a multinational to a transnational form.[2]

I must also state that Transco's parent corporation is considered highly successful even though the global restructuring caused a number of problems. One problem in particular, the successful development of local markets in a number of countries, required rectification in the early 2000s. Nonetheless, judging by most measures, *including diversity*, applied in studies by academics and others, the parent corporation receives high scores. However, the point here is precisely to look at a successful corporation that has a verifiable intention to diversify personnel as a strategy for excellence and to see why pitfalls for Japanese men and women, in the case of Transco, continue to exist. As corporate forms of globalization spread further, are there opportunities to review and revamp how people interact with one another across gender, nationality, race, and so on, or will corporations just extend the more opaque forms of American discriminatory practices outward?

Terminology and Related Issues

Some definitions are in order. The *transnational corporation (TNC)* goes beyond the *multinational corporation (MNC)* in both its complexity and its potential for ambiguity. On the one hand, the MNC has at least the expectation of a national and cultural center; the dispersal of subsidiaries is mainly geographic. On the other hand, the TNC ideally has no such center of cultural power. It is a hybrid form that crosses national and cultural divides, with each subsidiary as well as the original corporate headquarters feeling like the same entity. However, an emerging TNC likely clings to the more separatist (and comfortable) logic of the MNC, where each subsidiary looks toward the center and where, for example, an employee is either Japanese or American and working either in Japan or the United States. TNC logic would see that same employee as neither Japanese nor American and working globally.[3]

The expatriated managers at Transco understood TNC logic from a global production and coordination point of view but still cleaved to MNC thinking in their management of Transco's human resources. Claims of globalism in the corporate culture seemed to the Japanese employees to be little more than Americanism writ anew. This disparity forced a kind of chaos onto Transco: in social interaction at the company, culture became contested terrain in both overt and covert ways, and workplace interpretations of culture, gender, and authority were subject to the various manifestations of this contestation.

For a working definition of *culture,* I draw from a wide variety of sources.[4] Although there are no perfect cultural boundaries, culture is a system of beliefs, values, behaviors, symbols, meanings, and so on that are shared by members of a group, whether citizens of a nation or employees of a corporation. Culture is shared both consciously and unconsciously among group members; it forms the set of assumptions under which group members operate and delineates the strategies members use to interact with one another. Cultural transmission is relational and subject to constant change. Working together, "social structure and culture affect action and its consequences" (Chang 2004:410, on Mead 1934).

Culture is a troubling concept to many both within and without academia in large part because of its porous nature. This porosity leads to any number of problems; for example, employees at Transco often conflated culture and nationality, creating far more cultural homogeneity among national citizens than actually existed. However, rather than attempt to jump into the debates over the meaning and applicability of *culture* in and of itself, my intention is to show the ways in which culture was drawn upon by employees at Transco to create meaning and determine action. Culture provided them, rightly or wrongly, with a way to assess both their work and their personal lives.[5] Culture was thus salient for people at Transco.

Although the meaning of *gender* may seem clearer, it, too, requires some explanation as an analytic category, particularly because its misapplication at Transco usually stemmed from equating *gender* with *sex differences.* This misapplication is not a problem particular to Transco alone; academic theorists in a variety of fields, sociologists among them, apply *gender* and *sex differences* in conflicting ways that make cross-dialogue difficult.[6]

For the purposes of this book, *sex differences* are physiological, while *gender* is a social category. Unlike physical differences, gender, like culture, is learned behavior.[7] Our anatomy determines whether we will be socialized to behave like boys and men or girls and women as deemed appropriate by a given culture. Obviously, many of us stray from that socialization, but we continue to be judged on the basis of what is considered to be gender-appropriate behavior, most notably when we are either far inside or far outside the socially acceptable realm of appropriateness.

I agree wholeheartedly with Kimmel's (2000:4) assertion that "the differences between women and men are not to be nearly as great as are the differences among women or among men." He argues that gender difference is the result of gender inequality and not the other way around; to erase gender inequality is to make way for appreciation of individual qualities that are not rooted in gender. Culture works in much the same way: the differences among the Japanese or among the Americans at Transco were far greater than the differences between Japanese and Americans as a whole, but employees tended to focus on exaggerated differences between the two nationalized cultures in the same way that differences between genders were exaggerated.

Thus, in my research, *gender* and *culture* shared a number of usage patterns. All categories of people—men and women as well as Americans and Japanese—were imbued with seemingly immutable characteristics that were then used by both management and employees to justify a variety of decisions and behavioral strategies, including how authority was distributed both overtly and covertly. Misapplication of both *culture* and *gender* at Transco stemmed primarily from efforts to essentialize difference, to make sweeping claims about men, women, Americans, and Japanese, alone or in combination. Essentialisms then affected employee evaluations of themselves and others, both horizontally and vertically. However, because motivations for the use of these essentialisms differed from person to person, people counteracted one another on a regular basis without really knowing when or why, and chaos seemed to mark the corporate culture.

Cultural interaction served as both the cause and the effect of chaos. American and Japanese cultures came together to produce a new culture at Transco, but the new culture also superseded elements of Transco's corporate culture that senior American management thought it was setting in place. The significance of culture was more confusing to Japanese men, while Japanese women thought they had mastered culture, only to become confused about gender as they moved up in rank. Confusion over culture and gender lent further confusion to the meaning and performance of authority.

Last, the concept of *authority* needs to be separated from similar concepts, such as *power* and *influence*. Lenski ([1966] 1984) refers to *authority* as an enforceable right to command others, while *influence* is a more subtle ability to manipulate people based on one's resources and rights. Both are forms of institutionalized power, based on the *rule of right* and distinct from force (the *rule of might*); they are more socially acceptable and thus less subject to challenge; and they are more impersonal, being vested in the office or role rather than in the person. This distinction may be more applicable to men than to women, who lack the full range of opportunities to command as well as the personal resources necessary to influence people.

Weber ([1968] 1978) defines three ideal types of authority in terms of their source of legitimacy: legal, traditional, and charismatic. *Legal authority* rests on a secular belief in and support for established rules and the rights of those given authority by virtue of those rules; one believes in obedience to the established order and those who maintain it. *Traditional authority* derives its legitimacy from time-honored traditions; one owes loyalty to tradition and its keepers. *Charismatic authority* is awarded to the individual who is somehow exceptional enough to warrant devotion; personal trust in the vision of the charismatic individual warrants obedience.

Of the three types, legal authority may be the most susceptible to the vagaries of gender. Valian's (1999) work concludes that the "gender schema" for femininity is at odds with the schema for professional authority. Thus it is possible that women need to establish some amount of charismatic authority (such as exceptional capability or a charming personality) to buttress their legal authority, while men need only a single type of authority because male gender is a type of authority unto itself.

Weber distinguishes *power* from *authority* (which he interchanges with the term *domination*) in terms of agency. *Power* is the probability that a given actor will be able to carry out her or his will despite resistance; *authority* is the probability that a given individual or group will obey a command. He notes that "every genuine form of domination (authority) implies a minimum of voluntary compliance, that is, an *interest* (based on ulterior motives or genuine acceptance) in obedience" (1968:212). Thus an element of legitimacy becomes central to the reliability of a given authority, but again, female authority is generally regarded as less legitimate than male authority.[8]

Martin (1977) goes one step further in his determination that legitimacy (as "consent" on the part of a subordinate) allows coercion to be (partially) transformed into authority.[9] This constant interplay of superior and subordinate forces means that hierarchical relations are distinctly two-directional. But as Aron has noted, power is intrinsically asymmetrical: "When one commands the other obeys. In this sense, power can never be shared as wealth can be. Instead of the image of a marketplace with its competitors, there arises that of a hierarchy, of relations between superiors and inferiors, masters and servants (1988:77)."

However, within the context of gender and authority, the concepts of asymmetrical power and two-directional hierarchy must be considered further because different types of hierarchies and power relations occur depending upon whether or not the human relationships contained within them cross gender lines. Men do not question the authority of other men because of their gender, but they may well challenge women on this basis in at least a nonconscious way, if not a conscious one. Perceptions of gender differences in authority as natural are built into the schemas of gender and create the potential for gender discrimination in the competition for positions of authority.[10] Competitive discrimination allows the illusion of meritocracy to prevail without the dismantling of gender-based privilege in access to the ultimate authority that is prized in an organization.

The illusion of meritocracy may undermine women's workplace authority because it creates extended opportunities for culturally subjective comparisons of male and female managers that invariably leave women with less acceptance of their authority relative to men. In the early 1900s, women were excluded from career management in part because of the presumption of a fundamental incompatibility between their work and home obligations. We are now at a point where the compatibility is questioned less and women are given more career management opportunities, but for some reason women are still excluded from the highest positions in large numbers. By contrast, for a foreign firm in Japan such as Transco, utilizing women as a source of competitive advantage may significantly alter the realm of allowable comparisons between Japanese male and female employees.

Organizational theorists traditionally assumed that organizations were, by definition, gender neutral; later theorists came to view organizations as particular producers of gender relations[11] that differentially determine acceptable modes of workplace behavior and participation, ranging from emotional management[12] to access to technology.[13] Assumptions that institutionalized forms of power are more impersonal, drawing strength from the occupation of an office rather than the personal attributes of the officeholder,[14] do not hold up under the scrutiny of gender. If women are slower than men in attaining positions above the level of middle management, then personal, gender-based attributes would seem to be a factor in access to such power.

One's authority position at work was also found to explain a large portion of the gender gap in job autonomy, much more so than that explained by the gender composition of occupations.[15] We have also to consider the effects of women's roles as secretaries in the workplace and housewives/mothers in the home upon workplace attitudes toward women in authority. Historically, women's entry into career management was impeded by the perception that woman should remain at home or only serve in those positions that would not interfere with home responsibilities. And the gender status of secretarial work strengthens the assumption that women's role is to assist rather than to lead. This creates the potential for an additional barrier for women who attempt to position themselves as authority figures equal to men in the workplace. In sum, a relationship between gender and authority persists long after women have achieved the levels of education and experience necessary to occupy a place at the higher end of the occupational hierarchy.

Generally, women have been dismissed from earlier studies of power, perhaps because of the perception that they lacked any real form of either authority or power. This omission is problematic because of the amorphous massing of women into a single domain, but it also raises an interesting question concerning the effects of derived power (secondary power based on the power status of associated males) on the historical development of female authority in the workplace. As economic systems have been transformed from a more traditional, family-based form of capitalism to a more modern, managerial-based form, the avenues to authority changed for women, from family connections that often supersede gender to the false presumption of a meritocratic system that is gender blind.[16]

Though Transco's parent organization prides itself on being meritocratic along any number of vectors, the study of culture, gender, and authority patterns at Transco shows a picture of a transnational corporation roiling in a great deal of confusion and turmoil underneath a veneer of workplace precision and control. Confusion seemed to be most evident in Japanese efforts to negotiate the conflict between the American and Japanese cultures. Four cultural settings were reflected in the corporation: (1) the Americanized culture of the senior management and the mid-level expatriated management; (2) the Japanese culture representing the majority of the employees as well as the external national setting; (3) a mix of these two, within which individual employees negotiated personal solutions to their differential perspectives on the cultural conflict that arose between the first two; and (4) the corporate culture that was consciously designed through mission statements that outlined key principles and values, employee training programs, etc.

The confusion underneath the surface of smooth work relations also extended to gender. Some of the women who wanted to stay and build long-term careers were not doing well in the eyes of their expatriated superiors, while others who were deemed by senior management to be likely candidates for promotion did not seem to have much career attachment to the company. In between were women who were also trying consciously to do their jobs well, but they felt unsure about their place in the organization.

Cultural confusion for Japanese men was primarily over the tension between one's sense of value as a Japanese national and the Americanized values that seemed to prevail in the corporate culture. This confusion was exacerbated by the initiation of the globalization campaign that will be outlined further in the next section. Confusion for Japanese women was marked by this same cultural tension but was magnified and outdistanced by additional confusion over issues related to gender. These issues ranged from corporate expectations regarding negotiation of the conflict between women's work and home lives to whether or not so-called appropriate gender roles existed to differentiate the qualities of good female versus good male managers.

Women's assessment of gender roles included not only the subject of Japanese female managers but also the wives of the expatriated management, many of whom filled the more traditional role of a stay-at-home mother. In addition to negotiating how to be effective employees within the cultural tension that arose at work, Japanese women had to do so within a gender tension that emanated from both within and outside of the organization. They had ideas about how women in management ought to behave, but their expectations regarding Japanese women in management were confused by the conflict between the American and Japanese cultures and the gender conflict that arose separately within each culture. It seemed that Japanese women had more to contend with than did Japanese men, but the latter certainly had their own set of conflicts.

To assess the relationship between gender, culture, and authority at Transco requires the creation of a *typology of confusion* that addresses the types of confusion that are attributable (1) to cross-cultural perceptions, (2) to misunderstanding of workplace authority, or (3) to the sorts of gender imbalances that generally characterize numerous corporations and the contexts in which these three types occur. These three types of confusion and their related subsets comprise the chapters that follow.

Transco

Transco's parent corporation is a global heavyweight in market share for a number of its products, although it has had its ups and downs, particularly in the last several decades. It produces a wide variety of personal and household goods, many of which are recognized as global brands, and has operations in more than eighty countries. The net income of the corporation currently exceeds $8 billion annually.

Transco is an organization that relies heavily on both female and male Japanese employees in all divisions of the company, but senior management still remains mostly white, American, and male. Although employment patterns in Japan are changing, male graduates of the best universities still largely prefer to work for native government institutions and top-ranked corporations.[17] Thus Transco sees the potential for utilization of university-educated Japanese women as a key source of competitive advantage, a view that is augmented by the fact that Transco is a player in the competition for the loyalty of the highly discerning Japanese female consumer.[18] Japanese women were first brought into management at Transco in the 1970s as an experimental strategy to increase market share of specific female-oriented products. The numbers of women in management have grown steadily over the years, but they are still significantly lower than the numbers of Japanese men in management.

Table 1.1 PERCENTAGES OF WOMEN BY DEPARTMENT, 1997

Department	% of Women Overall	% of Women Managers	% Women not Secretarial	% Women Managers not Secretarial
Marketing	56.9	15.0	47.7	18.5
Human Res.	54.3	10.9	40.6	15.6
Finance	50.9	03.8	21.2	06.1
Info. Sys.	27.6	02.3	17.1	02.9
Legal	63.6	18.2	46.7	26.7
Mfg.	32.0	01.4	14.7	01.7
R&D	50.3	04.2	41.8	05.1
Sales	10.5	00.4	04.8	00.4
Other	76.6	12.8	66.7	18.2
Company	36.4	03.8	24.4	04.6

Source: Department of Human Resources, Transco

Table 1.1 shows the percentages of women in Transco's departments in 1997. A correlation exists between the number of women overall in a given category and the number in management within that same category. You will notice, however, that the correlation is weak and that certain departments were doing considerably better or worse than others in employing women. Even now, women managers at Transco are largely excluded from the more traditionally male domains of Finance, Information Systems, Manufacturing, Research and Development, and Sales.

Transco divides its data on the nationality of employees in Japan in multiple ways, with certain departments keeping much more comprehensive statistics than others. Overall, with the exception of Research and Development, which employs a significant number of non-Japanese at all levels, the employee population is overwhelmingly Japanese right up to the top of middle management, but there are multiple middle- and upper-level expatriated managers sent in and out of Japan for stints of two or more years.

At the time of my fieldwork, the top itself largely comprised white American males. Of the twenty-four most senior positions with direct ties to Japan (even if they have responsibilities for the Asian region), seventeen were white males, one was a white female, and one was a non-Japanese Asian male. Of the remaining five, four were Japanese males, and one was a Japanese female. Of these, two of the Japanese men and the sole Japanese woman, Ono-san, were targeted for removal from the organization. The men were considered "too traditionally Japanese" and Ono-san "too aggressive and immature" to continue serving in top positions.

Senior managers at Transco, however, viewed the company as very favorable toward both women and Japanese nationals. Transco claimed to hire capable Japanese men and women but saw the women as better performers overall, despite the fact that the women tended not to stay employed with the company as long as the men did. However, both men and women were thought to lack at least some of the qualities necessary to run the company at the top of the organization without help from the American side. The company was consciously looking for ways to redress two problems it viewed as inherent to the Japanese side of its managerial workforce:

(1) Japanese women's lack of commitment to long-term, upwardly mobile careers; and (2) an inability, on the part of both Japanese men and women, to develop the nontechnical skills, such as leadership style, deemed "appropriate" to senior levels of management as defined by the Americans.

Transco competes in Japan for sales of household and personal products marketed primarily to women. At the time of my initial fieldwork, several of Transco's products were experiencing a decline in market share. As part of its so-called lost decade, Japan took an economic downturn, and numerous product categories at Transco were struggling to make gains. Additionally, a corporate-wide drive, spearheaded by Transco's world headquarters in the United States, initiated a new campaign of globalization. A negative reaction to globalization reverberated especially loudly throughout the Japanese organization, with most of the Japanese employees feeling at least somewhat threatened by the campaign.

Exactly what the parent corporation meant by *globalization* was unclear to many employees at Transco, especially the Japanese. In being handed down from world headquarters as a new principle of operation, it was indeed vague. Implementation was intended to be large scale, encompassing standardization of everything from global packaging (to create greater economies of scale) and global brand recognition, to the creation of "global employees" marked by their common understanding of corporate principles and values no matter their geographic location. Local markets and local people were de-emphasized in favor of a new, seemingly "global" point of view that the parent organization viewed as a progressive step in its own development beyond multinational competition.

Globalization, or rather its precise definition and the implications for Japan, was often the source of conflict at meetings I observed. The perception of the unique character of the Japanese market was much stronger among Japanese at Transco than among their foreign counterparts, both in and outside of Japan. Decisions that were deemed good for global operations, such as global packaging, were feared to be bad for Japan because of a belief in the unique character of the Japanese market. Indeed, top American personnel at Transco often made the claim that to succeed in Japan was to succeed anywhere. Those Japanese in charge of the domestic market commonly reported feelings of being misunderstood by those non-Japanese in charge of global operations, including people at world headquarters in the United States as well as the expatriated management located in Japan and East Asia, Transco's primary sphere of operation.

An important point of gender difference that emerged from the study is that Japanese men were much more inclined than their female counterparts to consider globalization a personal threat to their sense of self and place at Transco. For many of the Japanese men, *globalization* represented a nebulous, higher power that was out there rearranging things beyond the authority range of the individual employee. Japanese men viewed the ramifications, particularly the negative ones, of Transco's implementation of globalization as being rooted in American culture, and as a result, during interviews they engaged in numerous comparisons of Japanese and American cultures, with Japanese culture deemed the superior one.

Japanese women, as previously stated, were not as concerned about globalization as were Japanese men. Although they were quick to agree with the dominant sentiment that globalization was bad for Japan, it seemed more a reflexive belief—shared by many Japanese—in the uniqueness of Japan and was not, by and large, as personally unsettling to them as to the men. Of note is the fact that, when they engaged in cultural comparisons between Japan and the United States in terms of men at Transco, American men were the clear winners. Not one woman I interviewed felt that her work life would have progressed better at a native Japanese corporation. Thus Japanese women were predisposed, at least initially, to favor the corporation and its Americanized culture, while perhaps Japanese men considered what they might have missed by not working for a native company.

Japanese women in management at Transco viewed gender as a workplace issue; while both newer and more experienced female managers focused on the potential for conflicts between home and work, the women with more experience at Transco also engaged in gendered analyses of the company. However, because all Japanese female managers believed that Transco treated them far better than any other option available to them in Japan, their perceptions of gender differences at Transco often were softened by this cultural comparison. Japanese women chose Transco, as an American company, in order to receive fair treatment relative to men. They came to the company with hopes for a promising career unfettered by the limited expectations of Japanese men and by the limiting views of Japanese culture toward women. As they advanced in the ranks, however, the tendency to frame perceptions of their work environment in gendered ways also increased, in large part because senior management itself was doing the same thing.

Beyond the expected discussion of conflicts between work and home lives that characterized interviews with newer women in management, more senior women often were acutely aware of how women in departments other than their own were doing, that is, which departments were considered to be woman-friendly and which were not. That women were aware of differences in how women were faring at the company makes it likely that gender mattered to individual success at Transco, and it was also a factor in individual commitment to a career trajectory in terms of both length of tenure and the type of work one wished to do. Women, for example, were more likely than men to request transfers to jobs with less strenuous career paths even when they were single and willing to devote long hours to work.

As mentioned previously, besides trying to get more women to commit to a career, Transco was also trying to develop its Japanese employees of both genders into an ideal type of leader, based on a variety of factors deemed by the senior expatriated management to be most essential. The ideal type was not considered to be particularly culture neutral because senior managers at both Transco and world headquarters (and elsewhere, presumably) saw many aspects of the American character as essential to the company's success, and these same people felt that the company overall had a history of strong success, though not without some bumps along the way.

What senior managers thought of as neutral was the application of the ideal; that once taught and knowledgeable, every employee around the globe should be able to fit the ideal. The "ideal employee" also became synonymous with the "global employee" envisioned in the globalization campaign. One paradox was that the Americans seemed least able to see the inadequacy of their own efforts at cultural adaptation precisely because the model was so Americanized. In many ways they were judging transnational employees based on their ability to at least mimic American behavior, but the rhetoric of the ideal employee was based on what was "best" for the corporation given the assumption of its record of success.

Cultural considerations came strongly into view, with Transco's senior American management dividing up desirable and undesirable traits along nationality lines. Desired traits such as creativity were considered more American, while undesirable traits such as a preference for rules were considered more Japanese. Over time it seemed that such distinctions were more likely to create additional blinders to assessment of individual achievement rather than promote understanding of the ideal employee.

Global standardization efforts accentuated these distinctions not only because of the sense of unease about the ramifications for the local Japanese market that the initiative fostered, but also because the emerging definition of the *global employee* seemed not much different from the American employee the Japanese had come to know. As such, to many Japanese, especially the men, it was highly suspect and laden with dangerous undertones regarding attitudes toward Japanese culture. The fact that globalization was just getting under way as a corporate directive renewed and intensified preexisting debates about the merits and shortcomings of the American and the Japanese cultures. Some debates were antagonistic, but many were not, and of course, all relied on stereotypes to varying degrees.

Transco is an excellent subject for the study of men and women at work in a transnational corporation. It offers a unique opportunity to look for the continued presence of and intersections between cultural and gender-based barriers to advancement into positions of authority. It is a company that at present is seeking to circumvent the vagaries of national cultures by actively creating a global corporate culture; and it is a company that has long touted its favorable attitude toward women. In Japan there is further inducement to promote women as a competitive strategy. Therefore, we can look at the Japanese men and women who have made it to the middle and upper levels and see what they think and how they are doing; and we can look at the expatriated management's view of them.

As a company for career-oriented women in Japan, Transco falls somewhere in between the idealized, meritocratic corporation that it considers itself to be and its more traditional Japanese counterpart. On the whole, Japanese women at Transco moved farther and faster than their peers in a native Japanese corporation. As they moved up, however, they became dissatisfied with the assistance they received from their superiors, both Japanese and American. Japanese male employees had concerns about cultural discrepancies at the corporation, especially those related to evaluation of one's worth as a competent employee destined to rise up the corporate ladder. They became even more concerned when globalization appeared on the scene as the new strategic directive. Globalization complicated their assessments of their own value.

By tracing the patterns of interaction between employees that emerged from contests over gender, culture, and authority at Transco, it is possible to address the types of problems that prevent transnational corporations from realizing truly meritocratic forms at all levels of the organization. Even when considerable improvement occurs in the advancement of women and local employees, cultural and gender biases can still prevail, providing blocks to one's establishment of workplace authority.

The Research Setting

Transco has a central administrative office along with several factories and scattered sales offices in Japan. Its corporate headquarters are housed in an impressive high-rise building that affords sweeping views of the area in its extensive use of glass. The ground floor entrance contains on one side a vast open space that is used for a variety of social and business functions; on the other side, a reception area that leads to a series of elevators; and beyond those, a large auditorium. The building mostly is divided by work function (R&D, Finance, etc.); thus little hierarchy is demonstrated by floor with the express exception of the top floor. It houses the most senior executives, those who run the company rather than all or part of a floor.[19]

Single floors reflect corporate hierarchy by means of private offices and personal windows with a view. Upper-level managers have corner offices, whereas the more rank and file share the remaining open space. It is interesting to note that Transco headquarters used to divide open space with a greater number of private cubicles, but when the company was forced to relocate temporarily to a more open, Japanese-style office while its building was undergoing earthquake retrofitting, people noticed that the work atmosphere seemed to improve. Thus when the company returned to its own building, management created more open space.

Every day employees pass by one or two receptionists in the reception area, display their identification badges to the guard, and proceed to the elevators. This, too, became part of my daily routine. Even though the building was large, company growth put space at a premium. Nevertheless, the company generously provided me with a desk, computer, and phone (including voice messaging) at one end of a conference room on the top floor; in addition, I was often given access to an office/conference room down a few floors in one of my key observation areas. Secretaries on both floors provided assistance to ensure that these two rooms were at my disposal as much as possible. As a result, I had a quiet place to conduct interviews with people who did not have their own office and to write up my field notes on those rare occasions when I had free time during my ten-hour days at the company. I started each day by riding to the top floor and checking for messages before proceeding through the day's schedule.

Ethnographers of American and other companies sometimes note the deafening silence on the top executive floor in comparison to the other floors; although it was indeed quiet on Transco's top floor, I did not find the other floors to be markedly less so. What was more pronounced for me was the feeling of isolation from the rest of the company on the top floor. In addition, there was a sense of loneliness to the floor itself. Unlike most of the rest of the floors where you opened the main glass door onto a large room full of visible people, on the top floor you simply walked along an oblong-shaped hallway that had private offices to the outside and conference rooms to the inside. Each of the top executives (all Western and male) had an executive, bilingual secretary (all Japanese and female) who was situated in her own office just outside his office. Except when the secretaries were away on an errand, their doors were usually open, but most of the other doors were closed, including those of the conference rooms. It was an odd feeling for me each day to take the long ride up the elevator and walk the seemingly deserted hall to my door. Though not an employee, I felt much more comfortable out on the open floors below.

Methodology and Introduction to the Key Informants

This study is based on research conducted in Japan primarily between 1996 and 1999, with some shorter trips that followed. Tracing the undercurrents of gender and cultural differences at Transco involved extensive observations of meetings both large and small, from the strictly work-related to the more ceremonial. For these meetings, I focused on two main departments: Marketing, and Research and Development. Both have very different subcultures and numbers of women in management, with Marketing having by far the greater share. The nature of these two departments is such that, especially in the case of Marketing, meetings I observed regularly included people from a number of other departments throughout the company, such as Finance, Manufacturing, Sales, Human Resources, and General Management.

Included in these observations were training sessions for both newer and older employees from any department, self-development seminars targeted to women in general, one out-of-town trip to visit customers with a senior female executive, and numerous social gatherings. Meetings and training sessions tended to be conducted in Japanese when all of the attendees were Japanese nationals and in English whenever non-Japanese were present, but there were some exceptions, as in the case of higher-level Japanese employees trying to advance their English language skills. Thus I was able to witness a great variety of people and undertakings and to compare people's behavior across languages.

To research questions on gender and authority, the case of Ono-san, mentioned previously as the most senior Japanese female, needed to be compared to other managerial employees. In consultation with Walter, the American at the helm of Transco, I chose six primary subjects, including Ono-san, for a total of two men and four women whose positions ranged from the first rung of middle management to Ono-san on the first rung of senior management. Following these six people around day after day afforded me unlimited access to all areas and levels of the company because, as stated previously, their two departments (Marketing, and Research and Development) have the most contact with other departments and personnel. I was exposed to countless meetings, a few ceremonies, a number of training programs, and contact with hundreds of employees, regularly including those at the top of the organization. Most of the time I was an observer, trying to make my (note-taking) presence felt as little as possible, but I became a participant observer for two training programs designed for various women in management.

The six primary subjects I chose were free to decline my request to observe them, but none of them did. Of the four in Marketing, three were women. Watanabe-san (brand manager) was a beginning manager of a single product; she led the only all-women team in Marketing. She was in her early thirties, single, had majored in American history at college, spent one year in Iowa as an undergraduate, and lived with her parents. She enjoyed her job but still had other career options outside of Transco on her mind, and she wanted to marry and raise a family. Her English language skills were excellent, and she displayed a confident but gentle style. Since her subordinates were newer to Transco, their team meetings were always held in Japanese and were among the most low-key that I witnessed at the company, but she herself also appeared low-key at meetings with her superiors. These meetings were held in English if a non-Japanese manager were present.

Igawa-san (marketing director) was a manager of multiple products and teams, including that of Watanabe-san. She was in her late thirties, single, majored in English in college, spent one year in Australia on a scholarship, and lived with her parents, though she, too, wanted to get married and have children. At all of her meetings I attended, no matter the language used or the size of the meeting, Igawa-san's style was quiet and gentle. In English, she also relied on humor at multiple points, taking opportunities for jokes as they occurred to her but delivering them in the same quiet manner. She appeared confident and relaxed, although I later came to learn from her that she did not like the intense pressures of Marketing and was considering a job change within the organization as part of her next performance review.

Ono-san (general manager), the first Japanese woman to enter senior management, had responsibility for an entire division. Both Igawa-san and Watanabe-san were her subordinates, and she thought highly of both of them. Ono-san was in her mid-forties, majored in English in college, and spent one year in England while an undergraduate. She had been married but did not have children; she was currently divorced and lived alone. She was, no doubt, the most forceful personality of the six, often speaking over her subordinates, gesticulating a great deal, and losing her temper on occasion. Of the six, she was the most stridently devoted to Transco. Because she was the one person marked for removal from the company and because she held an unprecedented location in the company hierarchy, additional attention will be paid to her case.

The fourth subject in Marketing, Abe-san (marketing manager), was a man in charge of multiple products and teams. He was in his late thirties, married, and had one child. Although he spoke English with a fair degree of accuracy, it was heavily accented to the point that his direct superior, a Canadian, remarked on it to me.[20] Abe-san's style was very quiet, quieter than either Igawa-san's or Watanabe-san's. He spoke in soft tones whether in English or Japanese and always seemed serious. Just prior to my first meeting Abe-san, this same superior described Abe-san as "very Japanese" in that, in addition to being quiet, he was reserved and careful, with a "Japanese sense of time" and too much of a "hands-off" attitude with his subordinates. However, he also told me that Abe-san was tagged for promotion to General Management pending successful completion of an overseas assignment. Abe-san did not want to leave Japan for personal reasons but knew that further career mobility depended on it; he was hoping to be sent to China.

Subjects in Research and Development were one man, Nobu-san, and one woman, Okura-san, both associate directors in their early forties. Each had similar levels of responsibility in middle management on the nontechnical side but had an academic background in chemistry. (Research and Development also has a technical track for employees who wish to remain research-oriented with little or no management responsibilities.) Both were married, and both had children.

Nobu-san had been with the company for more than sixteen years, and he became an associate director in 1994. After working at Transco for three years, he was sent to the United States for six months of English language and cultural training, followed by eighteen months at corporate headquarters working on a Japan-related project. Upon his return to Transco, he changed product categories within Research and Development a number of times and steadily moved up in management responsibilities. Compared to Abe-san, who always wore a suit, Nobu-san dressed casually but in good taste. I mention this because when I asked him to describe his idea of life in a Japanese company, he said the *ningen kankei* (human relations) there involved "how to wear clothes" and "how to deal with people," things that he feels are important but too restrictively defined in the traditional corporate context. Stylistically, Nobu-san seemed neither noisy nor quiet; either way, he gave the impression of being his own person and had a life outside of Transco involving his passion for music.

Okura-san described herself first and foremost as a "working mom"; her daughter lived with her because the husband/father's job necessitated that he live in Tokyo. She claimed never to have possessed a strong attachment to a career at Transco, opting instead to take a more wait-and-see attitude. Even before the birth of her child, she ranked family over work, leaving the office at five o'clock despite the general practice of people staying far later than that. In fact, she had a bit of company notoriety among the Japanese for her "early" departures from work; this was the subject of some amount of gossip. In my observations of her, I thought her personality was rather strong, not to the extent of Ono-san's but strong nonetheless, and she was not hesitant to appear dissatisfied with subordinates who did not do things the way she thought they should have been done or who wasted time. She was regarded highly by senior management, especially by her direct superior, an American known to have a rather volatile personality, and she enjoyed working for him.

All six of the primary subjects were considered to be successful, upwardly mobile employees, with the important exception of Ono-san. Table 1.2 presents basic data about each of the six subjects.

I conducted personal interviews with fifty employees, ranging from secretaries to top management. Essentially I asked everyone with whom I had frequent contact if they would mind being interviewed. I interviewed half of them more than once. The time frames ranged from thirty minutes to two or more hours. I recorded the interviews and took notes. The format generally was semistructured, and the choice of English or Japanese (or both) was left to the discretion of the interviewee.

I always started with a few questions and then let the interview take what seemed to be its natural course. If the interviewee touched upon a topic that paralleled something raised by someone else, I made sure to return to the topic at an appropriate point. Often I asked interviewees to restate their ideas in the other language in order to check for consistency of meaning. No one turned down my request for an interview. On a couple of occasions, I received

Table 1.2 THE SIX PRIMARY SUBJECTS

Name	Title	Division	Gender	Age	Marital Status
Ono-san	General Manager	Marketing	Female	40s	Divorced
Igawa-san	Marketing Director	Marketing	Female	30s	Single
Abe-san	Marketing Manager	Marketing	Male	30s	Married
Watanabe-san	Brand Manager	Marketing	Female	30s	Single
Okura-san	Associate Director	R&D	Female	40s	Married
Nobu-san	Associate Director	R&D	Male	40s	Married

phone calls from people who asked to be interviewed. They were concerned that I was getting a picture of the company that was "too positive" and thought I needed to hear their particular perspective on things.

American Issues in Gender, Culture, and Authority: Ono-san as a Special Case

In an article written for a major magazine, McDonald (2001) claimed that Linda Wachner, chief executive officer (CEO) of apparel-maker Warnaco, was dubbed the "iron maiden of lingerie."[21] The piece ostensibly was about the meteoric rise and fall of male as well as female CEOs in the difficult economy of the time, and the marked increase—up to 45 percent—in the personal reputation of a CEO as a factor in the overall reputation of the corporation that he or she guides.

Of the several examples of struggling CEOs given, all were women, with the "iron maiden" leading the pack. According to the article, Wachner's "aggressive management style" had once been considered a key component of Warnaco's return to manufacturing prominence, despite recognition of her seemingly volatile personality; but five years later as Warnaco struggled financially, "the very qualities that once won her kudos came under fire." At one time the "nation's highest paid female executive," Wachner had responded to critics of her compensation package by saying, "I get paid to be tough." From there, the article stated that "at the time, Wachner had reason for feeling smug." *The Economist* ended its own article on Wachner's downfall by saying that the collapse of her "empire" and subsequent loss of her own as well as shareholder investment "would, perhaps, be a fitting end to such a tale—but one that, unfortunately, will only hinder the cause of those female executives whose brightest role model she once was" ("The Wrong Trousers," June 16–22, 2001, p. 68).

A certain teleological approach is evident in these articles. Wachner's recent failure explains everything that came before, and it is intimated that her job failure is attributable partly to her personal failure to stay within the acceptable bounds of her gender.

The articles displayed a poorly hidden tone of delight over her fall from grace, with the assumption that her "tough" and "smug" style led to her comeuppance. Her story seemed to be presented as a warning to all women executives and represents a pattern that continues to this day. Though more sympathetic in tone, the *New York Times* report on the firing of Zoe Cruz from Morgan Stanley in late November 2007 bears many parallels to the stories provided on Wachner.[22]

The case of Ono-san also parallels the stories about Wachner and other top women executives. She had the longest tenure (twenty years) of any woman at the company and had been remarkably successful in the Marketing Department, achieving notoriety even in Japan at large for some of her earlier marketing campaigns. She was the highest-ranked and highest-paid Japanese female executive, not only at Transco but also, for a time, in Japan as a whole. Nevertheless, like Linda Wachner, she was in the process of being shown the proverbial door, her "large" ego and "tough" temperament no longer acceptable to the American senior managers with whom she was now working directly.

As in the Wachner case, Ono-san's temper did not go unnoticed by those working around her but was largely ignored over the years by her American superiors until she appeared to struggle at the higher levels of the job, meaning that profits in her division were down. As long as her job performance was seen as clearly profitable to the company and as long as the upper echelons of senior management were sheltered from constant contact with her, she was not only allowed to continue working but was regularly promoted into jobs of increasing responsibility over both people and products. Her performance, as it related to corporate profitability, was stellar until shortly before the time of my fieldwork. Her personality, however, had always been the same. By her own account of her history at the company, she had received occasional guidance in "proper" leadership behavior, yet she was not considered unsuitable to lead until her division saw a strong decline in market share and she had moved up in rank high enough to have regular contact with senior management in both Japan and the United States.

Since market share was itself never characterized by continual gain without any hint of decline and since other divisions were also struggling in the difficult Japanese economy of the time, there seemed to be more to the story of Ono-san's impending exit from the company than these factors. I thought that the best place to start an inquiry would be her relationships with senior management, particularly since I was interested in exploring, as one part of the fieldwork, whether or not the authority of managerial Japanese women translated fully to the top levels of a transnational corporation. From the very first day on site, I was presented with the case of a Japanese woman who had achieved more than any other Japanese, male or female, at the company, but one who was now subject to negative evaluation on virtually all fronts—most notably from those with the power to decide her fate.

No one in senior management complained about her negotiation of the dual culture in evidence at the transnational company; she was not criticized for being "too Japanese" as was the case for some of the senior Japanese men who were also going to be moved out of the company. Neither Ono-san nor these Japanese men were considered "good leaders" by the American management—the difference was that the men seemed to have cultural problems while Ono-san had gender problems. Thus their respective situations needed to be compared to other Japanese employees, both female and male, along the vectors of both gender and culture.

The corporation at large had an established set of operating principles that had been developed at parent headquarters in the United States and distributed to all its subsidiaries. These constituted the necessary values for effective on-the-job performance and were intended to be the basis of the corporate culture worldwide. Although everyone operated as if they understood the ground rules for employee excellence in both workplace performance and relationships with coworkers, in reality the rules were laden with mixed messages, and they were interpreted differently from person to person.

Ono-san's case is important precisely because she appeared to have lost her status as an excellent employee, a status she had clearly enjoyed until quite recently. I wanted to know whether her current problems could be attributed (1) to her role as a pioneer woman at Transco who was now considered somewhat outmoded, (2) to her own personality and nothing more, or (3) to "predictable" changes in senior management's opinion of her. Her case represents a microcosmic portrayal of the relationship between gender, culture, and authority, but one that reflects inconsistencies in the management of human resources at Transco.

Chapter 2 describes the key groups of employees at Transco and what they chose to share with me during open-ended interviews about Transco as a place to work, with comparisons to employment and organizational issues in Japan and the United States. Chapter 3 details the ways in which employees tried to define their selves within the context of the organization. Chapter 4 looks at the ways in which both culture and gender confused people's perceptions of themselves and others, and how culture and gender could be used as evaluative weapons in a variety of ways. Chapter 5 provides data on confusion in communication of authority across both culture and gender divides. Chapter 6 offers some conclusions.

All names and certain nonessential data have been changed or omitted to protect the privacy of the organization and the individuals who work there. I am, however, following the custom at Transco in regard to people's names. The Japanese employees are referred to in the standard Japanese way, by last name with -*san* (our equivalent of Miss, Mr., Mrs., and Ms. rolled into one) attached to the end, while the foreigners in general and the Americans in particular were referred to by their first names only, reflecting the preference for informality that Transco inherits from its American origins. This was accepted by both sides as the best way to handle the cultural difference.

For ease of reader recognition of my six key subjects, I will use their last names in full (for example, Watanabe-san) while providing only the first initial of a last name (for example, K-san) to denote other Japanese employees discussed in the text. All Americans will be noted by their first names.

All Japanese terms that appear in this work follow the modi-fied Hepburn system for romanization, with macrons denoting long vowels, except for commonly recognized terms, such as place names, and citations in which the author uses a different system.

2 Setting Transco within the Contexts of American and Japanese Corporations

The organizational mix of employees at Transco contains many categories. The top of the organization comprises mostly white males expatriated from the United States. In middle management Japanese of both genders predominate, but there are also a few expatriated female and male managers sent in for two- to four-year stints. Employees in R&D who focus mainly on research, clerks from all divisions, and secretaries who are not bilingual have the least contact with expatriated management.

My research focuses on the four categories of employees who have the most cross-cultural interaction: (1) expatriated managers (EMs), (2) Japanese men in management, (3) Japanese women in management, and (4) Japanese bilingual female secretaries. In this chapter I will first present an overview of gender issues in both Japanese and American organizations to provide the reader with some points for comparison to Transco, and then I will offer some general employee characterizations of Transco as a place to work and to have a career trajectory, before I move on to the detailed ethnography provided in Chapters 3 through 5.

Japanese Contexts

Historically, Japan was characterized by the highest rate of female labor-force participation in the industrialized world, owing mainly to the confluence of agriculture and family-run businesses.[1] The female labor-force participation rate in the United States did not surpass that of Japan until 1975.[2] However, within the last couple of decades, the rate for Japan has leveled off to around 50 percent,[3] while the rate has continued to increase elsewhere.[4]

The so-called rational economic strategy in the Japanese corporation offers some explanation for the leveling off. In the achievement of a corporation's balance between competitive and cooperative advantage, the careful choice of external competitors matched with orchestration of the internally cooperative environment necessary to compete successfully against them, Japanese women are a trade-off.

When Japan was riding the high tide of economic success in the 1970s and 1980s, numerous analyses of the successful Japanese corporation appeared, stressing features such as their chosen "competitive fundamentals" of

- A growth bias
- A preoccupation with actions of competitors
- The creation and ruthless exploitation of competitive advantage
- The choice of corporate financial and personnel policies that are economically consistent with all of the preceding.[5]

Although not stated as such, these competitive fundamentals include the maintenance of a highly cooperative internal environment based on the management of human resources as a core competency. The characterization of Japanese business strategy as human-resources-driven in contrast to the capital-driven American strategy[6] can be an oversimplification at times; nonetheless, it is true that the differences in the allocation of labor and capital led to two types of economic and corporate systems.[7] The human resources model in Japan, however, is one that employs women, usually part-time[8] for such things as electronics assembly and computer programming, but underemploys women in management in order to overemploy men.

Numerous sources, including the Japanese Ministry of Labor, can be called upon to support the contention that native Japanese firms rely on the exploitation of women as a distinct component of their business strategy. For one thing, the employment of women is seen as a buffer to economic downturn. The recession following the 1973 oil shock resulted in the adoption of an on-the-spot labor cost adjustment strategy based on the dismissal of large numbers of female employees[9]; since 1975 this strategy has become a permanent feature of the employment system. During the "lost decade" of the 1990s, predictably, women were hired in increasing numbers into nonstandard work (i.e., temporary, part-time, or contract) that paid much less and offered no benefits in order to shelter corporate profits; these types of problems continue to this day.[10]

In addition, the personnel system of lifetime employment and seniority-based promotions[11] sets up an irresolvable competition between women and men, where the creation of career opportunities for the former would translate directly into loss of career opportunities for the latter.[12] However, some scholars have argued against this assessment, believing instead that there is room for women in at least lower administration, as evidenced by the following fact:

> The Japanese system of organization and management features a narrow span of control, with an average of 5 to 15 people under one direct supervisor at each level. The consequent abundance of supervisory positions, plus the practice of foisting excess managers off onto lower-ranked subsidiaries, makes it possible to provide sufficient positions in the main administrative ranks for the entire age cohort of permanent managerial class employees. (Steinhoff and Tanaka 1993:29)

Although more women are in lower managerial positions[13] than before, overall the percentage of managerial women in Japanese firms is very small[14] and their rates of pay are both lower than men's and decline over time.

Justifications for these inequities often are blatantly gendered, with seemingly little change in attitude. A 2005 survey, for example, showed that human resource managers were still listing women's lack of experience as well as their *general lack of abilities* as major reasons for their continuing absence from management positions.[15] Even with the increase in merit-based systems of reward since the so-called lost decade, or perhaps because of it, companies still deny women opportunities to advance their skills and careers in order to placate men.

The Equal Employment Opportunity Law (EEOL) of 1986 was not much of a motivation for change. Because nonstandard employment for the majority of women workers is an accepted mechanism for short-term labor adjustment, the long-term (national) costs of underutilization of women as an employment resource is weighed against short-term (corporate) needs. When we couple this economic reality with cultural tendencies to allocate the spheres of home and work separately to women and men as a natural division of labor, the task of integrating women fully into employment becomes monumental.

The original corporate response to the EEOL was the creation of three employment tracks: *ippanshoku* (generalist, denoting mainly clerical work), *senmonshoku* (assigned to those with special technical expertise), and *sōgōshoku* (signaling work that involves decision making and designated for management careers). The vast majority of women are still assigned to *ippanshoku* status and are expected to remain with the company only until marriage; the vast majority of men are assigned to *sōgōshoku* and are expected to make a permanent commitment. And the Japanese government has little coercive power[16] to remedy the situation.[17] It does, however, try to set examples by its own policies toward female administrators, but this effort applies only to some sectors of the national bureaucracy.

Thus the track system of employment is ultimately an adaptation of older devices that contribute to maintenance of the status quo. It serves to eliminate some of the political pressure from both domestic and international fronts (feminist politicking in Japan was influential in efforts during the United Nations Decade on

Women to coerce the Japanese government into signing a United Nations Treaty on Women's Rights), but it also does little more than promote a small group of elite women while maintaining a system of promotion that is primarily beneficial to men and unavailable to non-elites who are mostly women.[18]

The argument persists that these policies are rational economically, but are they? At the macroeconomic level, the costs of prejudice against women as a potential resource are very high in the general Asian context[19]; and perhaps nowhere more so than in the Japanese context, where the continual underutilization of (secondary and postsecondary) educated women constitutes a huge loss to the national economy.[20]

At the microeconomic level, the lack of improvement in working conditions for women needs to be compared to the strategic response to growing differences between older and younger employees, especially in technical fields. Resignation of younger, technical personnel, such as engineers, is on the rise because of dissatisfaction with seniority-based wages and promotions that do not honor the merits of technological know-how obtained by the younger employees.[21] Seniority-based rewards have come under continual review since the 1980s and are giving way to merit-based rewards in order "to cope with further change, including the aging of the work force, slower economic growth and the diversified values of young employees" (Tomita 1991), but women's values do not seem to be part of the review.[22]

If the successful Japanese corporation produces alternatives to the seniority system as society continues to age in Japan, then better employment of females may come to outweigh the trade-off in cost.[23] Because there is currently a perceived need for certain forms of structural inequality, the adaptive, "rational" strategies of the 1980s confirm rather than deny sex roles[24] in order to hang onto a system that is favorable to, and valued by, male employees. Despite an increase in mid-career job hopping among Japanese men in management,[25] these types of sex-role strategies continue because, culturally, certain forms of discrimination against women remain acceptable.

In contrast to the native firm, the foreign firm in Japan (theoretically) should have a vested interest in utilizing the full capacities of women employees as a source of both competitive and cooperative advantage. The hiring of women directly compensates for the Japanese male preference for the better native firms; often women are the main source of employees with a first-rate, postsecondary education.[26] Many of these are career-minded women who largely have been unable to find employment commensurate with their abilities in the native Japanese firm. In general, the returns to education for women in Japan are negative,[27] but it is likely that a study limited to foreign firms would show positive returns.

In addition to the very large numbers of women who work part-time[28] in Japan,[29] most women work in small- and medium-sized enterprises that do not boast the same perquisites available in the large-sized enterprises that employ the so-called salary men. Takahashi (1998) lists this as one reason why the gender gap in earnings increases with employee age.

In assessing Japanese women's employment opportunities within firms, both Lam (1992) and Takahashi (1998) consider the effects of the EEOL for their analysis. Although Takahashi is somewhat more optimistic given amendments to the law in 1997 (effective 1999), both argue that the EEOL as originally devised was of limited value in helping women to achieve managerial status. Most of the provisions were not mandatory, and the potentially hostile work atmosphere for women was not addressed.

Takahashi[30] describes some of the problems mentioned by the first post-EEOL generation of professional women:

> Many believed that their male colleagues considered them to be curiosities. Large numbers also felt pressure to earn their superiors' praise and to set a good example, fearing that, otherwise, successive generations of women entering the job market would feel betrayed. Male managers often were clumsy at integrating female white-collar workers into their teams, and the clerical staff typically resented the new women professionals. The frustrations proved too great for

many, and they changed employers or even stopped working. Up to 70 percent of the women graduates of Tokyo's prestigious Hitotsubashi University who took professional-level jobs in 1986 left their original employers.

Although this first generation of post-EEOL women professionals was bound to suffer more than subsequent generations, the EEOL came to be widely regarded as a weak effort to improve the work lives of women. Of note, however, is that the severe downturn in the Japanese economy of the late 1990s has decreased the numbers of new workers hired, with female college graduates among those hit the hardest, and the rhetoric of the primacy of women's role in the home rose again[31] and continues today.

As a complement to that rhetoric, the traditional Japanese view holds that generally women should not assume the role of authority figure or business decision maker.[32] Cultural assumptions in Japan predict trouble if women supervise men. In 1987, a poll conducted by the Prime Minister's Office reported that 70 percent of Japanese men were unwilling to work under a woman supervisor.[33] Twenty years later, Sakata (2007) states: "Given the current situation in Japan, one must admit that it is extremely hard for women to develop a work career which includes a managerial occupation in its scope" (p. 58). In the more impersonal world created by the large, nonfamily corporation, perceived gender differences are generally interpreted as constituting limiting frameworks within which female authority is circumscribed in a radical manner.

For women in positions of authority, the right to express authority is contested on a variety of fronts. On-the-job performance pressure, perhaps one manifestation of culture, causes women managers in Japan to lower the pitch of their voices and drop superfluous syllables from their speech to suit masculine definitions of professionalism.[34] For some Japanese women, however, traditional female speech becomes a specific strategy for being heard.[35] And despite that numerous terms denigrating women are being phased out of usage in the mass media and official government documents in Japan, many remain. In general, "control over women through language is still significant."[36]

Despite efforts to fit in, statistics on native Japanese firms reveal continued resistance to the promotion of Japanese women to management (*sōgōshoku*) status: in the 1990s, women generally comprised 1 percent of *buchō* (division or department chief), 3 percent of *kachō* (section chief), and 6 percent of *kakarichō* (chief clerk, the lowest-level management position); only small increases have occurred since then.[37]

Additionally, the attrition rate among *sōgōshoku* women approaches 50 percent.[38] Given that males dominate the authority hierarchy, their preferences are likely to prevail in both organizational structure and culture, causing difficulty for female employees. For example, women who achieve assignment to the management track in major Japanese corporations are under considerable pressure from all sides to refrain from marriage and children. Companies argue that their investment in women executives will otherwise be wasted, still believing in a fundamental incompatibility between the responsibilities of home and office.

Employment conditions in Japan may have been driving Japanese women to seek work with foreign firms. Japanese media representations of both statistical evidence and cultural assessments of problems associated with Japanese women working at native firms certainly provided women with ready-made reasons why things had to be better at a foreign firm. Yet Transco women claimed that a few other reasons also had to exist for them to want to apply to a foreign firm, such as a desire to work directly with foreigners and have opportunities to use English. Once hired by Transco, Japanese women began to stress the benefits of the American firm in particular.

American Contexts

Although the American context is one in which claims of statistical and cultural superiority in the treatment of working women are often made, particularly in comparison to Japan, the "rationality" of the American corporation still evades full meritocracy. It is possible to argue that as the historical underpinning of bureaucratic organization, traditional (Weberian) theories are seriously inadequate from a gender perspective and have skewed the possibilities for progress. Weber saw the ideal type of bureaucracy as perfectly rationalized, with authority emanating from the office itself rather than the person occupying the office. Although he was concerned primarily with the function of bureaucracy in society rather than organizations per se, it nonetheless seems ill advised to divorce any bureaucracy, even one in an ideal form, from the culture in which it is operant.

Witz and Savage (1992: 9) propose that "any common patterns of organizing are due not to any technical, functional imperatives but rather to the common embodiment of particular forms of social and power relations within them." New approaches to organizational structure incorporate women as necessarily subordinate employees in both work arrangements and reward systems,[39] which contributes to the growth of gendered organizational cultures.[40] For example, the assignation of females to the role of cheap labor, the segregation of workers by sex, and the preservation of a male-dominated hierarchy all manifest a workplace ideology based on a belief in innate gender differences. Even in those areas where women's participation in the workforce has increased substantially, such as the service sector of the U.S. economy, these basic patterns of gender organization have not changed to any large extent.[41] Change occurs, but very slowly.

Boundaries, as set by physical separation of the sexes and by differentiation of access to the various levels of organizational hierarchy, serve as social controls that constrain individual assessment and aspiration.[42] The organizational structure and culture work together to reinforce existing boundaries of behavior and control. Stories such as the ones about Linda Wachner related in Chapter 1 outline where those gender boundaries are supposed to be, and organizations serve as sites for socialization.[43]

Perhaps women in American firms can aspire to positions of authority more readily than women in Japanese firms; such aspirations may be *expected* of these women in cases such as Transco, given the greater willingness to invest in female employees as part of a specific business strategy. However, considerable evidence exists over time that men also resist the authority of women in the

American context for a variety of organizations[44] and that support for this kind of resistance can be found in the personnel practices of employers.[45] The Japanese case thus seems less specific to any intrinsic differences in nationality; the differences, while important, are matters of degree.

Another important debate concerns the existence (or not) of gender differences in management style. Beyond the behavior described by Kanter (1977) as that of "tokens" and "dominants" rather than "females" or "males" (see Chapter 6 for further details), do gender differences persist? Nonverbal gender differences, for example, are said to be quite robust,[46] and

> persistent findings indicate that females are superior to males in sending and judging the meanings of nonverbal cues, and that they have more expressive faces, smile and laugh more, gaze more, approach others more closely, touch others more, and exhibit fewer speech disturbances than males do. . . . In sum, based on a literature of hundreds of studies, it appears that women occupy a more nonverbally conscious, positive, and interpersonally engaged world than men do. (Hall and Halberstadt 1986:137)

These types of differences between men and women can create tension in mixed sex authority relations and lead to a double standard for women, who are expected to be more emotional at the same time that they are punished for it as an undesirable workplace trait.[47]

Statistically, the American corporation, along with organizations in general, is still marked by the glacial pace of women's entry into senior management levels. In the report, "A Solid Investment: Making Full Use of the Nation's Human Capital," made public in 1995 by the federally mandated Glass Ceiling Commission, Chair Robert B. Reich noted the persistence of workplace discrimination against the higher-level advancement of women and minorities in the United States.[48] Five years later, the numeric data remained virtually the same, with some improvement thereafter, but still requiring four to five decades for women to catch up. The commission noted that, as a general rule, less than 5 percent of the senior managers in any of the major business categories (i.e., Fortune 500 companies, Fortune 1000 industrial companies, Fortune 2000 industrial and service companies) are women or minorities, despite the fact that 57 percent of workers are women, or members of minorities, or both. The report goes on to recommend a variety of unsurprising strategies—commitment to diversity, use of affirmative action as a selection tool, promotion and retention of qualified individuals, and so on—and calls on the federal government itself to lead by example.

Were it not for the element of time, this report, which itself was three years in the making, might be a gauntlet cast as a first step toward real change in the creation of full equality of employment opportunity for women. In actuality, however, the report only serves to verify the lack of change that continues from year to year, and from decade to decade. For example, one can refer to a 1980 study by the Organization for Economic Co-operation and Development (OECD) that examined affluent capitalist countries and determined a pattern of women's underrepresentation in administrative and managerial occupations and overrepresentation in clerical and service occupations in all of the subject countries. Going forward to 2008, *Human Resource Executive Online* reports on two studies that respectively show that women's desire for senior management positions decreases the longer they are in the workforce, likely due to increased recognition that the playing field is not level, and that the low numbers of women currently in senior management is due primarily to barriers to entry.[49]

Perhaps understanding the persistent lack of certain types of change for women who work outside the home, in particular the continued absence of women from senior management positions in either the public or private spheres, requires a new approach. Rather than focusing on the tools necessary to break through the glass ceiling, it may be prudent to explore further the reasons for its relative impermeability by looking for the specific needs—economic, cultural, or social—that its existence fulfills.

At the level of the glass ceiling, the stratification system becomes distinctly more rigid and is increasingly correlated with a gender-based hierarchy. Within the overwhelming majority of countries, capitalist and otherwise, women are denied full access to a variety of "male" domains, most of which represent the loci of power within a particular area (business, the military, etc.).[50]

Since we know that socialist countries have fared little better in dismantling such a hierarchy, the system of economic organization probably is not the most central problem. But different systems, including subsystems within capitalism, may serve either to promote or to mitigate certain features of gender discrimination. Economic organization is a product of human values; "rational" economic decisions are defined by "cultural" norms. In the intersection between economy and culture, then, social institutions such as gender are created.

Transco's Contexts

Within the larger environment where studies suggest (1) that Japan is, indeed, a worse place than the United States for women to strive for management careers, but also (2) that the United States still produces considerable barriers to women's entry to senior management positions, how is Transco viewed by its female employees, and what comparisons can be drawn to its male employees? Was the corporate culture reflective of these studies or did it serve as an alternative to them?

When management women of any nationality characterized the corporate culture at my request, they tended to use terms that mark human-to-human relationships rather than those between an organization and a person. For example, women often described Transco as "honest" while no male informants did. This choice of terminology is in keeping with women's preference for a more interpersonal work environment as shown by the studies mentioned earlier in this chapter, whether as a function of gender socialization or not.

Transco as a whole received high marks from women as a place that treated women well. Particularly in comparison to their ideas of how things work at native Japanese corporations, though few had any direct experience, Transco was considered truly enlightened.[51]

Women often spoke of the company as being "fair" or even "equal" in its treatment of female employees relative to men on any number of vectors, including compensation.[52] Other management women also mentioned the flexibility of rules as one company strength, citing the requirement for changing rules simply to be management support and marking the flexibility as "the beauty of this company."

Though women perceived conflicting messages from the top level of management in terms of women's access to the top, they did not necessarily view the messages as discrimination based on gender unless they had to deal with these messages directly, as was the case with Ono-san. Since women were not yet in senior management positions, given that the requisite passage of time was just completed for Ono-san as the oldest female executive, most interviewees cited the fact that senior executives (all of whom were Western and male at the time) had wives who did not work outside of the home. This observation was not taken as proof that women had a slim chance of making it to the uppermost tiers in the company as much as proof that those positions rendered the people in them completely incapable of contributing to the daily management of a home. Rather than seeing discrimination taking place, women tended to individuate their perceptions of top management and themselves: they saw the excessive time commitment as fundamental to those top jobs; and particularly if they wanted to marry and have a family, they had no desire to have a job where a full home life simply was not possible.

On the subject of gender and work, a connection can be made to assessments by a number of women's groups in Japan that are less rooted in equity than their American counterparts, or at least present the solution to equity differently. Some Japanese feminists have long made the argument that the structure of male employment, with its excessively long hours and "company as family" ideology, needs a complete overhaul; it is not healthy for either men or women to subscribe to such norms, and the structure must be addressed before female employment opportunities and advancement can realistically improve.[53]

Another related issue was the kind of women whom upwardly bound male executives, both American and Japanese, at Transco were perceived to prefer as wives. The terms *onna-rashii* (very lady-like and feminine) and "female female" were used, usually to describe women who were quite unlike the women who worked at Transco, the latter simply being "women." Again the thinking was not so much that "ladies" are inferior to "women" as it was that there is no equivalent spousal match for women who want to move up the corporate ladder; to move up was to resign oneself to being single, and most women did not want to do so even as they matured well past the presumed upper limits of marriageable age in Japan.[54]

Perhaps what is different about the Japanese women in management is that they rarely blamed either the company or society. Many stated that they would like to find a male partner who was able to understand his wife's need for a career, but women still perceived a huge conflict of time and energy when it came to managing a home and a career. Their home responsibilities would not allow for the kind of time devotion they saw in the senior management males. These beliefs were and are in keeping with those in the larger Japanese society.

By no means were the employee-driven perceptions of the corporate culture all positives. One recurrent source of tension was the belief widely held by both Japanese men and women, especially in areas of greater day-to-day pressure, such as Marketing, that the company adhered to an "up or out" philosophy where one either continued to be promoted or left the company under some duress. This belief was by no means lacking in credibility; the head of Transco told me that it was, in fact, true for Marketing, as is common to many companies, but not necessarily true for other divisions even though the Japanese employees believed it to be so. In the difficult economy of the lost decade, paranoia over losing one's job increased markedly. The legal prohibition on firing employees in Japan did have a different twist at Transco; whereas Japanese companies have a reputation for moving ineffectual employees to the proverbial broom closet, Transco tried to convince certain employees to leave the company of their own volition.

Other angles to corporate characterizations were based on perceptions of cultural differences between Japan and the United States. One important perception was that Transco was *honne* rather than *tatemae* in orientation, that is, a company that supported true expression rather than a false public persona, and women held this belief to be part of Transco's overall honesty. The *tatemae/honne* dichotomy is a weighty cultural signifier in Japan of which even young school children are aware. *Tatemae* refers to expression of a publicly acceptable position, while *honne* refers to one's real feelings; essentially the difference is in the level of openness with which one can say what one really thinks or feels. School children, by the time they join school clubs in middle school, distinguish between best friends with whom they can be *honne* at all times and participation in clubs which requires the display of *tatemae* to other members in order to be an appropriate member at all times.[55] This eventually translates to the world of work, among many other areas of life.

Employees evaluated *tatemae* and *honne* from a number of perspectives. As mentioned, women often introduced the concepts of *tatemae* and *honne* as part of their discussion of Transco's more honest, straightforward character. As Watanabe-san explained it,

> [the type of *tatemae* that I think is right is] the *tatemae* which can help human relationships, or help communication, or help the work to proceed. That type of productive *tatemae*, I try to use it. But when I say this company is *honne*, more *honne*-based, to me it means that this company does not have any rule for nothing. I tend to think that Japanese people or Japanese companies have many rules, which do not necessarily have some reasonable or logical explanation why you have to do it. And I really hate those types of *tatemae*.

This statement is reflective of general employee sentiment. Transco was seen as a place where you did not have to worry so much about subordinating yourself to the dominant sentiment or method of doing things. Rules did not exist for the sake of having them, and people were free to define how they handled their work and to develop their own individual style. Japanese women in particular felt freed up by the more *honne*-like atmosphere, and their preference for *honne* is one reason why they initially conformed to the culture of Transco more readily than Japanese men. In particular, the older men were more likely to see some benefits to *tatemae* as a way to maintain good relations between people who occupy different rungs on the corporate ladder. However, younger men such as Nobu-san (who did not want to be told "how to wear clothes") were more oriented toward *honne,* while those like Abe-san tried to strike a balance between the two.

The senior American management at Transco believed that the corporate culture was still too *tatemae* in orientation. Some tried consciously to push Japanese employees toward *honne* and away from *tatemae,* believing that *tatemae* damaged employee relations and stifled creative work output. They wanted to move to what they saw as a more American model in which employees feel free to disagree with their superiors and go forward with ideas even if they seem risky or silly.

Gender and Career Satisfaction

Stories that women in their forties told about their earlier work histories at Transco revolved around the theme of helpful American male management in contradistinction to the Japanese men in management at the time. The following exchange with Okura-san illustrates this view:

> OKURA-SAN: I was so lucky working for several EMs. The international managers had matured more [as managers] and also they didn't have any discrimination [against my] being a female.
> INTERVIEWER: You didn't see any at all?
> OKURA-SAN: For Japanese men, I saw it, but for EMs I did not. Actually, I was lucky. I just reported to the EM who eventually became a director. In the second year after I joined the company, he was promoted. He was a mentor for me, so whenever I had an issue he really taught me how to [handle] it. And he was so broad in thinking— he just gave me a chance to go to the U.S. for a one-year

assignment with my daughter and I'm sure a Japanese
manager would not have even thought about that kind
of opportunity for me. But what he said was, "There is
an opportunity—do you want to wait until your kid becomes eighteen years old?" Well, probably not. And
then he told me to just go and look for daycare and
everything in the States; he just sent me [there to] see if
it was viable or not. . . . Meeting him was the change in
my career.

Women with longer tenure at Transco consistently spoke of past
associations with American male mentors as being instrumental to
their development of a career orientation, even if they arrived at the
company without such intentions. Interestingly, this type of men-
toring was not true for the younger women in management whom
I interviewed, and the older women felt that things had changed
for the worse in this regard. The latter's stories of the early years
(1970s and 1980s) reflect the time period when Transco initially
made the (then-experimental) decision to hire and promote Japanese women as a source of competitive advantage. The atmosphere
at the time was one in which people attended to implementing the
change with an eye toward anticipating women's needs.

Now the company is used to women, which may have both
positive and negative consequences. On the positive side, a more
critical mass of women exists from which to select candidates for
further promotion in the future. And the greater number of
women working in management ensures that feelings of isolation
are rare at least in certain departments. However, where women
once received special treatment, they are now considered to be on
a par with men, and the perception of parity decreases the likelihood of the kind of special treatment to which the older women
fondly referred. In recent years women have become increasingly
dissatisfied with the career guidance they have been receiving as
they advance in their careers, particularly when compared to men.

As an employee advances, he or she may be recommended for
further training, which in Transco's case would include English
language proficiency as well as advanced seminars on how to be a

more effective manager. Generally, training programs are geared more toward skills acquisition than toward helping employees envision a long-term place for themselves in the company, in which they move, perhaps slowly, but certainly steadily, up the ranks. One reason is that an employee's vision of her or his career trajectory in the organization was supposed to be developed in consultation with superiors during personnel reviews.

Employee review on at least an annual basis is one common method of evaluation and consideration for promotion. Annual reviews were the practice at Transco; employees wrote up self-assessments that included further career plans, and their immediate supervisor evaluated their performance for the previous year. Some supervisors took this responsibility much more seriously than others, and there were problems with efforts to rationalize the criteria of reviews and promotions. Although many employees found these annual reviews to be helpful, many did not, and on the whole, women were much less satisfied with them than were the men. A very common complaint among women was specifically that the reviews did little to help them see where they were going in the corporation, despite the fact that career planning was an integral part of the process.

In terms of overall satisfaction with both their employment and their employer, Japanese women managers repeatedly score higher than their male counterparts from year to year. However, these same women score consistently and significantly lower than the men when it comes to satisfaction with performance evaluations and career guidance from their immediate superiors. Table 2.1 summarizes data on the satisfaction of men and women employees at the three levels of middle management at Transco over three separate years.

Compared to their male counterparts, managerial Japanese women grow more satisfied with both their career and the company as they advance to upper-middle management but more dissatisfied with any type of guidance they are receiving. Generally, women in middle and lower management weigh in on the same positive or negative side as women in upper management but not to the same degree. Potentially, this difference represents the change

Table 2.1 WOMEN VERSUS MEN ON SATISFACTION

	1993		1996		1998	
	Women	Men	Women	Men	Women	Men
Overall Satisfied with the Company—% Yes						
Upper	—	—	92	80	86	76
Middle	69	56	51	45	61	52
Lower	52	39	33	29	38	38
Satisfied with Individual Job—% Yes						
Upper	—	—	92	81	93	83
Middle	81	75	53	51	62	55
Lower	55	45	35	33	42	41
Satisfied with Career Development—% Yes						
Upper	—	—	100	73	79	72
Middle	60	56	48	43	61	47
Lower	38	27	25	25	27	27
Receiving Good Career Guidance—% Yes						
Upper	—	—	33	54	50	60
Middle	31	41	33	46	45	53
Lower	38	44	35	47	38	47
Evaluation Provides Clear Steps for Performance Improvement—% Yes						
Upper	—	—	45	65	43	75
Middle	—	—	41	57	59	65
Lower	—	—	40	51	49	56
Satisfied with Work/family Balance—% Yes						
Upper	—	—	08	44	50	61
Middle	19	44	20	42	24	39
Lower	42	53	51	39	40	42

Source: Transco supplied the data for this table.

from the early years of encouragement described by the older female employees, when they were fewer in number and part of a conscientious effort to foster managerial women.

One might also make the case that work and family conflicts come into play more as women move up the corporate ladder, but there is evidence to the contrary in two ways. First, in terms of satisfaction with work/family balance, the numbers are not as consistent as the other data, showing large swings over the three sample years. These variations indicate the possibility of changes in family situation from year to year but not necessarily with a corresponding change in satisfaction at work. However, the recognition that motherhood was one of the most time-consuming occupations that a woman could have in Japan no doubt influenced women's thinking about work/family balance since most women at Transco wanted to get married and raise a family.[56]

Second, and more important, at the time of this research, management women were more likely to be single than married, and upper-management women were the most likely to be single of all.[57] Overall, 63.0 percent of management women were single, compared to 30.3 percent married (and 6.7 percent divorced or widowed). At the upper level, 83.3 percent were single, while 16.0 percent were married (0.7 percent divorced). For all management men, the single ranks made up only 23.2 percent, while married men constituted 75 percent (1.8 percent divorced or widowed). For upper-management women then, dissatisfaction with evaluations and career guidance is likely situated primarily in the workplace rather than in conflicts between work and home. And it is strongest among women who are opting for a career over marriage and family; thus the women who are devoting themselves most fully to work are the ones most likely to feel dissatisfied with the career advice they receive from their superiors.

Interviews highlight some possible explanations for women's greater dissatisfaction with the evaluation process. Women with considerable tenure at the company often said the annual review was not helpful, responding to the pertinent interview question with a resounding "No!" in English or a Japanese equivalent. The following are some of their complaints:

> It's just a talk, a write-up talk of my strengths and weaknesses. If they think that talk is fixing it [they're wrong]. It would be better to send people to outside seminars or schools to help with weakness areas. . . . This system expects people to capture meticulously [market share] year after year, but there's no actual help. Also, we drill too much into weaknesses and don't praise strengths. (Ono-san)

> It's just used for calibration purposes. Calibration is very strange; it's done by people who don't know me or my work, so it's a power game. If the objective is to recognize my achievement and my work, my boss should know this

already. It's probably a good tool to mutually align expectations and desires, but it's not so helpful with future career
goals. If I could [change the process] the company would
give meaningful support to pursue the next step and prom-
ise a career path. (M-san, market research manager)

Rationalization of criteria, as can be found in the "calibration" re-
mark, is an important point: evaluation of the pioneer women at
Transco used to be more personal with an eye toward encouraging
them to continue on a career path. Transco viewed the results of
the satisfaction survey with some concern, marking the coaching
of women as a specific area for improvement. One solution was to
bring in two women's development programs from the United
States, both of which will be outlined in Chapter 4.

The complaints of women are similar to the typical complaints
made by Japanese men who are unhappy with the evaluation process. During interviews, the men, though fewer in number, also
stressed the lack of visionary help with one's place in the organization and a belief that the process was performed in a vacuum, lacking recognition that performance was wholly dependent upon any
number of changes beyond their control in both the internal and
external environments.

Those men and women who did find the annual review helpful
stressed gaining confidence from positive reviews and a clearer understanding of the next steps they should be taking, particularly if
they were lower-level managers. Even among this group, however, I
was likely to hear from women that the evaluations did not help with
career vision. For women in upper management, the next steps to
take to improve one's performance become increasingly nebulous,
as they do for men in upper management. As both genders move up
in the ranks, their work becomes less and less about the objective
tasks they perform and more and more about the subjective management of people under their leadership. But for men the results on
satisfaction are still significantly better concerning guidance from
superiors on what steps to take for improved performance.

Japanese men in management struggled with the seemingly
endless efforts on the part of Transco's parent corporation to

rationalize performance evaluations, which resulted in confusion for them in their roles as both subordinates receiving feedback and superiors providing feedback. Constant realignment of criteria of performance augmented a general perception of the American corporation as less stable than its Japanese counterpart. Nobu-san noted:

> But when it comes to some of the new personnel system, it's very difficult because, for example, our rating system has been changing every three to five years, and I am tired of always explaining why I am changing [it] because it's simply hard to explain. . . . And that typically happens, I think, in American companies rather than in the Japanese corporations [where] the moving is more gradual and the consistency is more valued. So if I see any value from the Japanese company, it's that kind of thing. People at least feel like there's good continuity, but in the American company people just have to understand that's how things go.

The freer atmosphere of Transco that Japanese women liked was viewed by Japanese men as synonymous with inconsistency on a number of points besides the personnel evaluations under discussion and the globalization drive that will be discussed in the next chapter. The continual development of business concepts for day-to-day operations as well as appropriate corporate principles and values often were said to be problematic. As Abe-san explained,

> upper-level managers tend to understand just the concept, but they don't fully understand the details and simply go down, take it down to the next level of managers as some task for them. And those managers also just understand the concept, but since they got that concept as an assignment, they feel they have to deliver some proof of what they did. So for them, sometimes it is not important to understand the concept fully—they just try to develop some outcomes, which often are not actionable, which often are not meaningful.

The important point to be made here is that Japanese employees of both genders regularly perceived a disconnection between organizational concepts and meaningfulness. Concepts are quite easy to dispense; agreeing on the meaning of those concepts and the appropriate steps required for implementation of them is much more difficult. Failure to do so, however, creates a constant source of uncertainty among employees. At Transco, this uncertainty seemed to increase as one moved up the corporate ladder.

It would seem that Transco is, thus far, fairly reflective of the studies on Japan and America outlined earlier in this chapter. Japanese women thought it was a far better option than a native Japanese corporation, and on many fronts, so did the bulk of Japanese men, especially younger men. But satisfaction with career guidance and performance evaluations was a problem area that grew proportionally worse for Japanese women as they advanced in rank, even though they continued to praise the company for its treatment of women. Japanese men tended to focus on dissatisfaction with implementation of company policies and concepts that seemed to change too often, impeding any sense of corporate continuity. Women seemed to trust the organization as a whole but not their personal interactions with their superiors, while men were more likely to express the opposite. In the more detailed ethnographic portions that follow this chapter, we will look at some of the reasons for this and other dichotomies.

3 Uncertainty, Trust, and Commitment: Defining the Self in Relation to Employment at Transco

There is little doubt that employees at Transco and elsewhere think about themselves in relation to their work organizations on a regular basis. Where choices are at least presumed to exist, employees analyze why one choice of a workplace is better than another, and corporations such as Transco spend considerable time and energy convincing both potential and existing employees why it is the best choice at different stages of their career trajectories.

Over time employees learn to trust, or not to trust, their company, based on a variety of factors that become more important as one moves up the corporate ladder: a personal sense of fit with the organization, some measure of predictability in regard to corporate expectations of employee performance, evidence that solid performance will lead to a continuing career path, and a belief that one understands both organizational objectives and the working concepts and principles behind those objectives.

This chapter further explores these factors. We already know from Chapter 2 that satisfaction with both career and company increased as Japanese men and women advanced in the organizational hierarchy, with women generally ranking these factors higher. However, in terms of satisfaction with career guidance and clarity of evaluations, women rank these factors far lower than men do. Given that career guidance and performance evaluations involve one-on-one interaction with an employee's superiors, some amount of personal uncertainty is likely generated in the process, and for women this form of uncertainty paralleled men's uncertainty with the corporation at large. Transco recognized women's career uncertainty as a problem, listing coaching of women as a specific target for improvement. The problem was that solutions were vague, for example, asking Human Resources to provide "appropriate support," and did not address the behavior of bosses directly. Nothing seemed to be in the offing to address men's uncertainty; I do not think that particular form of uncertainty was even recognized in any organization-wide way.

Efforts to rationalize further the criteria of either career advancement or effective implementation of concepts that flow down from the top of the corporation will not eliminate the problems because perfectly rational bureaucracy is impossible.[1] Organizations, large ones in particular, face uncertainty at all levels of operation on a daily basis. The need for personal discretion therefore becomes unavoidable and increases in intensity as one moves up the occupational hierarchy. Discretion, in turn, intensifies key *human* issues of trust, loyalty, commitment, mutual understanding and shared values that rarely rise in technical matters, all of which are in return reaffected by uncertainty:

> It is the uncertainty quotient in managerial work, as it has come to be defined in the large modern corporation, that causes management to become so socially restricting: to develop tight inner circles excluding social strangers; to keep control in the hands of socially homogenous peers; to stress conformity and insist upon a diffuse, unbounded loyalty; and to prefer ease of communication and thus social certainty over the strains of dealing with people who are 'different.' (Kanter 1977:49)

Kanter does make the important point that mutual trust can be established by means other than social homogeneity, in particular by a "similarity of organizational experience" (1977: 50), but the requisite time is much longer. We still can only hopefully assume that over time women's continued presence in an organization is likely to override considerations of gender. Yet, three decades after Kanter's book appeared, we were not yet there for managerial women in numbers that were commensurate with their presence in organizations as a whole, and the Japanese of either gender at Transco were not yet trusted to take the reins of the subsidiary despite their presence in the company for a similar period of time.

Mutual trust is said to be part of the "Japanese management creed" (Tomita 1991), but in this sense the trust appears to be as important along vertical lines as it is along horizontal lines. The necessity for vertical lines of trust may be in contrast to the Western corporation, where expectations of competency transfer along vertical lines, but expectations of personal trust are more important among peers within different levels than between levels. The primacy of horizontal lines of trust is one motivation for the increase in self-replication (Kanter's 1977 social homogeneity) as the corporate ladder rises.

The stress on "institutional affiliation rather than universal attribute" (Nakane 1970) suggests *groupism* as the term to use for the set of values embedded in the Japanese system of organization.[2] The Japanese corporation is said to be a different social institution in comparison to that of the West; the former is thought of as a family, based on an exchange of commitments between employer and employee as well as the extensive socialization of employees carried out by the corporation and the total involvement expected of them.[3]

In the Japanese view, the employment of women is a potential disruption of the system[4] because women are expected to manage the home to help facilitate men's devotion to work. Japanese women are beginning to argue for the creation of a new organizational culture that suits their needs and to promote this idea as a positive step for all employees. The existing culture, with its expectations of excessive overtime, after-hours socialization, and familial-type concern for the company, is considered bad for the physical and mental well-being of men as well as women, as mentioned in the previous chapter. Again, rather than moving women toward the "male standard" of employee behavior, many women believe the Japanese corporation should be moving everyone toward a "female standard," where work is less antithetical to home.[5] However, such a move is unlikely given management's primary focus on profit, job security, and the like.

The foreign firm provides the potential for the creation of a third, hybrid culture that combines the best elements from each country. In the case of Japan, there is the additional potential for solutions to many of the problems encountered by women working in native firms. The result "can be uniquely beneficial to the company in terms of increased commitment, participation, and stability of employees and employee-management relations" (Wakabayashi and Graen 1991:160). As Lincoln and Kalleberg (1990) point out, employee commitment to an organization is "a very powerful mechanism of control" (p. 23).

However, greater commitment to long-term careers on the part of women is something that Transco still struggles to achieve. As we shall see in the following section, a number of the management women hired by Transco described their personal sense of "difference" from the Japanese norm as one reason for their career orientation, but this difference was not necessarily embraced at the higher levels of management. For Japanese men, neither difference nor commitment seemed to be issues, but uncertainty in the face of globalization was.

Japanese Women in Management

During open-ended interviews, one of the most noticeable characteristics about Japanese women in management that set them apart from the other three categories of Transco employees was a tendency to describe feelings of being different as a child. Although these feelings ranged in scope from the moderate to the more extreme, they nonetheless shared in common the idea that these women were violating to some extent a strong Japanese norm for female behavior.[6] For some women, it was simply a point of observation about their lives and feelings, but for others, it was the source of considerable childhood angst. Part of their personal maturation was coming to grips with their sense of difference.

Watanabe-san, the woman who recently had entered the first rung of management, shared with me her sense of difference from the norm as a child:

> I went to a girls' [high] school and in those schools there are two typical types of groups. One is really female—"I want to just go to junior college and I want to get married as quickly as possible to a wealthy husband" type group; and the other type of group is more outgoing, trying to take leadership because there is no boy to take leadership, and I belonged to the latter. And in that group, people really, like my teachers, groomed my ambition, and a belief in myself, [but] also I felt [I had] a complex [about] the first type of girls [who] looked very girlish and who seemed like they were enjoying their lives. I know that I can't be in that group, but at the same time I kind of wanted to be in that group, so that type of complex made me think that I needed to be different and that I wanted to be different, and that I wanted to be in a place where I [can be different].

Parents figure prominently in these women's conception of themselves, especially in their willingness to go against the grain of expectations for both girls and women.[7] Even in cases where a girl's mother was regarded as a typical Japanese housewife, supposedly representing one of the most traditional groups in Japan,[8] the messages received from her were rooted in encouragement to take a different tack in life. Watanabe-san describes her mother as a "one hundred percent housewife" who nonetheless encouraged her to be on a career track. When asked about primary identification with a particular parent, she answered:

> I didn't really consciously compare myself [to my mother when I was young] or try to be different [from her]. I never did that before, but now I really think I am different and I cannot be like her. And I more tend to sympathize with my

father than my mother at this age, because I am more career-oriented, right, so I can sympathize with how my father behaved like this, [and] to me my mother sometimes looks a little childish because she doesn't know the outside world.

Watanabe-san went on to say that she believes her mother perhaps had similar, career-oriented aspirations when she was young, having performed very well in primary and secondary school. However, her life followed a trajectory common to Japanese women of the 1960s and 1970s, and Watanabe-san thought her mother was at least mildly frustrated with having taken this path. Rather than go to college, she attended a school for prospective brides (*hanayome gakkō*), worked as an *office lady (OL)*—the common term for secretaries—for two years, and then quit to get married.

Although *hanayome gakkō* are no longer common in Japan, the number of junior colleges has increased markedly, and they offer a feminized curricula to their mostly female students.[9] But even women who attend four-year colleges often follow the same path of work as an OL until marriage or childbearing. The main difference is that the age of marriage has risen such that time spent as an OL typically lasts two to three times longer than was the case with Watanabe-san's mother. In Watanabe-san's case, she was planning to have a long-term career, though she did not think that meant staying at Transco. She had yet to decide, but was toying with the idea of moving into social work.

Another woman on her way up the management ladder at Transco, K-san, told me that she always knew she did not want to be like her traditional stay-at-home mother. In fact, she described wanting to be a man until well into her late twenties. She majored in economics at a major university and originally planned to go to work for a large Japanese corporation. It was her major professor who advised her to seek work with a foreign company. Had she been a man, he told her, he could have placed her with an excellent Japanese company, but since she was a woman, he felt that her talents would be wasted there. Since he did not have any connections to foreign corporations, she had to strike out on her own. Thus she landed by chance at Transco.

Ono-san (the "Japanese Linda Wachner") describes herself as always having been different and happy to be so, in a rebellious kind of way. Other women were more likely to describe feelings of initial reluctance, when in high school, for example, to be different from the typical Japanese teenage girl. They viewed themselves as different from the mainstream but thought life would be easier if they were not. Later they came to accept their sense of difference, but Ono-san felt no remorse for her childhood:

ONO-SAN: In order to be different, I did all kinds of "bad" things [use of the term "bad" here refers to going against the grain of the group], just to be different. If a group of people is going this way—this is a silly example—even if it looks good, I may go that way. I'm not so good at ganging up for the sake of ganging up.

INTERVIEWER: From the time you were a child?

ONO-SAN: Yes. I could always speak up [as to] what's on my mind; I could always speak up [as to] what seemed to be right and wrong. In fact, I didn't care what others would think about me saying something before I said it, which in itself is not so typical. And I was raised always like that. So, in fact, I suffered a lot by being in a one hundred percent Japanese society, up until I spent one year in the UK after I finished the third year of university. I said, this is freedom—I can be anything and nobody is looking at me, because I may look different and I wanted to be different. The moment I went to London, I said people are different, different colors, their eyes are different colors, the color of the hair is different, opinions are different, different kinds of English, Italian English, Spanish English, American English, British English. It's all kinds of things and people *just go by*. What's wrong with being different? So I just relaxed. That was eye opening.

In detailing her experience of coming to terms with her own sense of difference, Ono-san is alluding to a powerful mechanism for social control in Japan, whereby pressure to conform to behavioral norms is applied, to children by parents, and to students by teachers once middle school begins.[10] Spending time alone is discouraged, while participation in sports and other clubs is adamantly encouraged; consequently, the child's memberships in a variety of groups come to characterize the self.[11]

Traveling with Ono-san on a number of work-related and other occasions, I observed that she was, in fact, watched by other Japanese in a way that I had not experienced in the company of other Japanese friends and acquaintances. Her manner is very direct, her speech forthright and not quiet, and she even carries her physical self in a more casual, open-bodied way that is unusual for both men and women in Japan, particularly women. I was more used to looking up and finding someone watching me as a foreigner, but with Ono-san, I always discovered them to be watching her.

Difference from the Japanese norm for women seemed to mark one aspect of management women's lives. Far more than bilingual secretaries, who seemed to be among the most comfortable Japanese women at Transco, some of the women in management struggled to gain a measure of congruity between their sense of self and their expected role as women in the larger Japanese society. In many cases, working for Transco allowed for this measure of congruity. Their difference was appreciated (up to a point), but their work also required expertise about their own country and culture. To some extent, they were able to feel better about themselves as Japanese women by working for Transco. The company provided them with a sense of place, and no one I interviewed could imagine themselves at a Japanese corporation. They were virtually universal in their view of Transco as the superior choice. When reviewing their personal work histories with me, women tended to stress the positive aspects, particularly in regard to gender, of work life at Transco.

Ono-san came specifically to Transco somewhat by accident. She was on the job market in Japan after returning from London and finishing her bachelor's degree. She already had concluded that a foreign company would be the better choice for a career with growth opportunities. She felt that a number of factors prevented her from finding meaningful employment with a Japanese company, beyond the "difference" factor highlighted above. One was taking five years to complete her undergraduate degree by including the year abroad, which according to Ono-san, was viewed as a negative. Little value was placed on the foreign experience she had gained, and it created suspicion toward her as potentially too individualistic. At least in the Japan of the 1970s when Ono-san came of age, considerably more value was placed on graduating with one's cohort as one sign of being a good prospect for employment. Second, she stated that women graduates of *kokuritsu daigaku* (national universities) were seen to be "more argumentative, or the negative way to describe being able to think, or being more logical perhaps, or analytical."

Transco happened at the time to be looking for Japanese women interested in a career in marketing. It was a decision based partially on the fact, still true today albeit much less so, that male graduates of the top Japanese universities prefer not to work for foreign companies, seeking instead employment with the Japanese government and top Japanese firms. The flip side of the coin is that it was and is still, but to a lesser extent, difficult for Japanese women to get good career opportunities with a native Japanese firm, even if they themselves are first-rate graduates of the best universities.[12] So Transco's decision to look for female applicants was based on their recognition of a new way to approach the supply and demand of labor in Japan. Thus Ono-san ended up with a position in Marketing at Transco.

She described the initial environment that she worked in as "nurturing" in that the expatriated managers took it upon themselves to train her in a very hands-on manner and closely monitor her progress. She saw the company as less nurturing during the time of my fieldwork, but continuing in this vein at least as measured by its willingness "to hire more women into any of the [divisions] than any other company in Japan, both Japanese and non-Japanese." Although the numbers of hires did show considerable difference based on division, this statement may or may not be true. Nonetheless, Ono-san was describing how many of the Japanese women at Transco felt about the company.

Ono-san started out at the lowest level of brand management, with an American EM as her direct superior. She had nothing but good things to say about him; indeed, many of the senior Japanese women that I interviewed were quick to credit their *earlier* EMs—American males in all cases—with their successful growth as company employees, in terms of both the performance of their day-to-day work and the expansion of their personal ideas about future career possibilities.

Despite the encouragement of EMs, much confusion existed about appropriate gender roles in the early days of women's entry into management at Transco. It was left up to the women themselves to sort things out. Ono-san described one situation that took some time to resolve:

ONO-SAN: I can tell you that when I joined the company, the context was such that managers—men—were prepared to have me, but who were not prepared to have me were the secretaries.

INTERVIEWER: When you first started here?

ONO-SAN: They [the secretaries] couldn't identify "my self"; basically they identified me as a new kind, but then said, okay, group her into the secretaries in terms of dishwashing, tea serving and stuff like this. One way in which my bosses did not help me out is that they left me to sort this through by myself. So I did not have help. Was I angry? No, I was so innocent in those days. Just by being hired into an international company, I was so happy. So I was involved in dishwashing, like, I am making this up, Mondays and Thursdays I needed to do dishwashing, and I needed to make tea or coffee. I needed to know exactly how many sugars that I had to put in, does this guy want his coffee with milk, all kinds of things. And I did go through these rituals and not say anything. I knew that the way I could get out was to show them that I could do the project and deliver the results, and these examples will convince them that I am a different kind. It took them quite a while, several months, to acknowledge that I am a brand assistant, . . . but by and large, they became very sympathetic toward my situation, and [it was] the secretaries who eased me out; it's not me, but they really chose to ease me out of this rotation.

Ono-san took it upon herself eventually to relieve even the secretaries of much of the burden of such menial chores. After she was promoted to brand manager, she worked to institute informal policies. She obtained approval for expenditure on paper cups and encouraged the men who did not want to use paper to wash their own cups. Tea-making continued for several years, but after Ono-san was promoted again, she sought expenditure for vending machines to provide hot and cold drinks. During my field research at Transco, some fifteen years after Ono-san's efforts, I rarely saw such services being provided to management below the top levels, and the cases that I did see seemed to be largely at the discretion of the secretary.

Despite a large number of Japanese women in management describing a sense of difference for themselves, not all of them felt this way. However, for the middle level and up of managerial women who had put in years of service at Transco, interviews showed a strong correlation between having this sense of difference and a desire to continue to build a long-term, upwardly mobile career. Women who did not struggle with difference tended either to have less career attachment to the company or planned to move to less stressful positions off the line to general management at some point in the future, but Watanabe-san was an exception.

As noted in Chapter 1, Okura-san, from R&D, was a working mother, a rarity among management women in any division at Transco. She worked at another American company before moving to Transco; she met her husband there, quitting upon marriage. Leaving the Japanese company upon marriage was and is still the common pattern for Japanese women, but in Okura-san's case, she felt uncomfortable even being at the same American company; she also used the time off to decide what else to do with her working life, as motherhood was not yet on her timetable. Obtaining a Ph.D.

was one option, which one of her friends was doing; getting a different job was another. She studied independently for a while, learning German in preparation for a doctoral program, but in a few months decided instead to reenter the job market. The friend getting the Ph.D. was in the process of turning down an offer from Transco, and Okura-san landed the job in her place. These types of connections, made in a major metropolitan area of Japan, are an indication of the dearth of women candidates for employment at Transco at the time (1970s and 1980s).

Because Okura-san was already married, she entered Transco with much more of a life outside of work. She cited her husband as a major influence on her attitude toward her job:

> My husband really influenced me a lot. He is really good at priority setting and doing things right—"if that is right, do it; if not, don't do it" kind of very pragmatic person, so I learned a lot from him. And that's why I didn't do any overtime work—I tried to work very hard during the daytime, and didn't do overtime. . . . I wanted to have my family every night; I wanted to have some happiness in my personal life, too. So I had no plan to destroy my family by working more from day one. . . . I didn't expect [to have] a career in front of me at that time. Because I'm a woman, and then [a woman with] a family, and it was very difficult to find any precedents either, so I didn't think that way [about having a career]. If something comes [to me], it's fortune, and if my performance is good, something may follow, but it's not something I tried to grab.

About one year after joining Transco, Okura-san had her first child. After taking maternity leave, she returned to work, continuing to give equal weight to home and work. She left work at five o'clock to pick up her daughter from day care and adhered firmly to her decision to work hard by day but leave work behind at night and on the weekends.

Igawa-san, marketing director, also was someone who did not feel particularly different as a child. While moving up the line toward general management, she increasingly leaned toward moving off the line into an expert (staff) position:

> The good thing (about) being in brand or working in the brand group, it really tells you in what areas the company expects you to grow, and [for] the long-term career, the company expects brand people to become general managers. They use a more factual way—they say more than 90 percent of general managers are out of brand groups. [This] doesn't deny there are GMs [general managers] from other functions. . . . That's why I think that this level is almost like a key milestone or key point where I make myself clear to the company whether I want to be a consumer expert or continue on, and they want me to continue on to general management and above. I don't think I can manage it. I don't like that strong business pressure.

As part of her yearly performance evaluation, Igawa-san had stated in her written plan that she had risen as far as she would like to go on the line and would prefer to move over to a consumer expert position that did not yet exist but that she hoped Transco would create for her. Even though she was not yet married, she cited both work/family balance and the pressures of responsibility for increasing profits as the two main reasons.

Japanese Men in Management

During interviews, Japanese men included neither references to childhood nor perceptions of difference from their peers in their stories, even when prompted. I suspect that "difference" did apply to some of them, but it was not an issue in their lives. Some of the women I interviewed thought that men were attracted to employment with Transco because of its emphasis on *jitsuryokushugi* ("ability-ism," which refers to a merit-based system) for promotion rather than the traditional additions of age and seniority found in Japanese companies. Women viewed this as one major distinction between Japanese men and women who came to work for Transco—

the men were motivated by the principle of *jitsuryokushugi*, while the women were motivated by the prospect of fair and equal treatment relative to men.

In open-ended interviews, Japanese men focused consistently on comparisons between American and Japanese culture. Japanese women, relative to Japanese men, were more positive toward American culture in general and the Americanized culture of Transco in particular. For Japanese men, the culture of Transco was presented primarily as a set of problems that tended to prevent optimum company performance.

These cultural problems were of several types, including consistent complaints that Americans did not speak Japanese or really understand Japan (see Chapter 4 for more details). The most prevalent complaints concerned issues of globalization, the major corporate drive at the time of my research at Transco. Globalization was of widespread concern to Japanese employees, extending to both men and women, but men were far more concerned about it as an obstacle to their individual sense of place in the company. Both genders expressed nationalized sentiments about globalization's capacity to diminish corporate understanding of Japan as an unusual and highly competitive market. This concern was logical in that many thought globalization would harm the successful operations of Transco in Japan. But women did not extend the effects of globalization to their personal sense of place at the company, while men did.

General ideological conflicts stemmed from the perception that globalization was antithetical to the particularistic needs of Japan as a consumer market. One of the objectives of globalization was to achieve economies of scale through global packaging and the like. Japanese employees of Transco, reflecting the attitudes contained within Japanese society at large, were convinced of the uniqueness of Japan and feared that Japanese consumer tastes could not be satisfied with any sort of global approach to products. Though these types of conflicts were not gender specific, it was men who shared them at length during interviews.

One of the corporate stories spread by Japanese employees accents the perceptions of Japan as a unique country from a number of angles. As mentioned previously, Transco had veered away from attempts to compete against Japanese companies on the latter's terms and instead chose to emphasize it's own (Americanized) strengths as an alternative in Japan. This emphasis augmented Japanese employees' belief that Japan was too unusual for any non-Japanese to understand it. Also, in the move away from playing a Japanese game, the company for a considerable time chose to stress the idea that success in the Japanese market was an indication of the ability to succeed anywhere on the planet, precisely because the market was so different. Winning in Japan became a sure sign of corporate ability worldwide, and this idea fit well with, indeed encouraged, the Japanese employees' sense of national pride.

Thus as *globalization* became the corporation's new motto, it threatened many of the assumptions under which the Japanese employees had been operating. It is also true that, even without this history, globalization was confusing. It came as a directive from above, but without clear indications as to how it would be carried out. People lower down would take the directive and add their individual interpretations to it, reflecting the personal discretion that uncertainty makes mandatory. With this interpretations came some indication as to methods and priorities, but these, too, could result in difficulties. Abe-san summed it up:

> ABE-SAN: [Once] the importance of Japan was recognized again, the global organization tried to understand the difference of Transco Japan. Unfortunately, all of us are still not sure how or what is the most effective way to realize or implement that [globalization] concept, and we are still repeating trial and error to fully implement that concept. Even if [the leadership] says Japan is different, or rather, if we cannot succeed in Japan we cannot succeed globally, [it] is not freely deployed down the entire organization. Even with Asia, other Asian countries don't care what is happening in Japan. That also may be true for R&D; they understand the concept but that doesn't mean they have to change their working style, because the concept is not systematized into the organization.

Abe-san's comments need to be compared to those of Nobu-san. At the time of my fieldwork, they worked in separate divisions (Marketing and Research and Development) and did not have regular contact with one another, but convey nearly identical opinions when it comes to Transco's implementation of concepts such as globalization:

> INTERVIEWER: How does one of these "extreme things" [Nobu-san's characterization of globalization] get conveyed through the company?
>
> NOBU-SAN: Clearly it comes down; someone at a high level gets the idea, "let's go global!," and then it spreads.
>
> INTERVIEWER: How does that happen?
>
> NOBU-SAN: It is coming from the top, top management, but then the next level of top management gives their own interpretation, and it tends to get even more, let's say, emphasized, and they try to make it more concrete. That means less leeway or flexibility to work with, and the principle starts to get the rules, and then it goes down. Of course, I'm not necessarily criticizing; I think for conveying the message Transco has a pretty good system and I think management at least has the capability to communicate the sort of direction the company is heading in, not hiding anything; it's pretty clear. But the flip side is, I think in the process the principle or direction starts to get more like a rule. And then the rule doesn't necessarily work in every situation, so people simply struggle over what to do with it.

Nobu-san's comments are particularly interesting in light of a comment made to me by the American head of Transco, Walter. He felt that one major problem with the culture of Transco was that the Japanese are rule-based, while Americans prefer principles. Yet Nobu-san felt constrained by the arbitrary rules of globalization that would result from unclear principles and the potential for the creation of rules that would not work in Japan. Globalization actually was more of a guiding principle, at least in the beginning, but its definition and the rules for implementation needed to be hammered out.

One criticism of Transco that came solely from Japanese men was rooted in the notion of *continuity* as a Japanese ideal. In a more traditional Japanese corporate system, it was said, continuity in both ideas and leadership was an important value that precluded the type of flux considered to have negative consequences at Transco. The age range of the men at Transco who felt this way was wide, from thirties to late fifties. Examples include Nobu-san and I-san, taken from separate interviews:

NOBU-SAN: The way I characterize it is, maybe one bad thing is, Transco, probably somewhat inherited from American culture, they tend to go to the extreme.

INTERVIEWER: In terms of what?

NOBU-SAN: In terms of everything. Everything. When something [seems] right, when somebody believes this is the right way of doing [something], it goes all the way. No sort of in-between or compromise or anything. It's like, this is the right thing to do; this is right, do it, just do it, kind of spirit. There are some cases where I see the benefit of doing so, but I think it also creates some inconsistency over time, particularly if somebody worked for the company for the last twenty years or so. Because I can see the company always shifting back and forth. . . ."

I-SAN: The company is making the same mistakes over and over. The problem is constant rotation—everything depends on the new leader and his "new" ideas. A Japanese leader would provide continuity, if allowed to remain in office. Especially in the last couple of years, employees don't have confidence, particularly in management. There is too much change, often going in opposite directions, then back again."

Part of the problem is the need to rerepresent oneself whenever a new expatriated manager arrives in Japan. As will be highlighted below in the case of bilingual secretaries and EMs, regular rotation of EMs in and out of Japan was regarded unfavorably by virtually every Japanese with whom I spoke. Though they may exist, I could not locate even one Japanese employee who saw this practice in a positive light.

From the company's viewpoint, rotation of EMs has considerable value in terms of both strengthening the capabilities of individual managers and providing a large talent pool from which needed slots can be filled. And part of the newer thinking about globalization was the idea that Transco would create "global managers" who, by definition, would be able to arrive at any office worldwide and be effective immediately. It was thought that standardization of procedures, albeit with some local adaptations, and a thoroughly global outlook on the part of the company at large would help foster global managers.

From the point of view of the Japanese male employee, he would just get used to one EM's "way of doing," only to have to start all over with the next EM. In all likelihood, this frequent need to adapt to a new superior was an issue of personal control. As EMs were rotated, they had different strengths and weaknesses and different likes and dislikes. One might do very well with one EM and less well with another for reasons that were not necessarily connected to one's effectiveness as an employee, indicating that very little, if anything, was truly standardized at the middle and upper levels of management.

To be sure, actual conflict was minimal. Transco claimed to select and promote employees very carefully. Interactions were centered around the job, and good employees generally did not cease to perform well under a new EM. But the negative attitude toward rotation of EMs was, as stated before, widespread among both Japanese men and women. To understand why, it is helpful to look from the viewpoint of bilingual secretaries, who worked most closely with EMs. By interrelating these two groups, I hope to highlight the characteristics of both.

Bilingual Secretaries and Expatriated Management

I chose to focus on bilingual secretaries because of their close association with the management elite. Their fluency in English, coupled with the nature of their secretarial status at Transco, makes them indispensable to EMs in particular but also to Japanese managers. They occupy a special place at Transco.

In her path-breaking book, *Men and Women of the Corporation* (1977), Rosabeth Moss Kanter depicts the secretaries of her anonymous company:

> For the secretaries themselves, there were tradeoffs involved in their position. Although they were subjected to the personal whim of their bosses rather than to impersonal rules and orders scrutinized for fairness, they also retained a direct and special relationship to a person they could influence and manipulate. They had only one or two people to please, rather than being enmeshed in the larger bureaucratic tangle, where they would have to manage multiple relationships to get ahead. Although they were rewarded for someone else's achievements and status rather than directly for their own talents and skills, they could also derive much closer contact with power and privilege than they could ever attain on their own. So for many secretaries, too, the personal, non-rationalized residue in their position made life in the corporate bureaucracy easier to live.

This description generally still fits a company like Transco, but discrepancies exist. The promotion of bilingual secretaries is ranked from Level 1 to Level 5, each level representing the requisite responsibilities associated with working for higher levels of management, but promotions were nonetheless heavily dependent upon the discretion of individual managers. At the time of my fieldwork, bilingual secretaries were aware of the disadvantages stemming from this discrepancy and were engaged in efforts to rationalize further both their work and managerial evaluations of it. They saw a gap between themselves and other categories of employees, for which work tasks and evaluations are at least presumed to be more objective. Interestingly, bilingual secretaries were attempting to rationalize evaluation of their performance at just the time that Japanese managers were complaining about continuing efforts to do the same for their performance. One key difference is that the secretaries were in charge of this process for themselves.

EMs are rotated frequently both in and out of Japan. It is extremely rare for an EM to arrive with more than a modicum of Japanese language training, though they have had some minimal exposure to the culture in a company-sponsored course. Once they arrive in Japan, language training is provided by the company, but most EMs do not move beyond the most elementary language skills. The time allotted to learn Japanese, approximately three hours per week, is insufficient for acquisition of this difficult language, even if an EM had the incentive. EMs also weigh the linguistic effort against the fact that they will be rotated out of Japan within a few years, as likely to another country as back to the United States.

Because EMs have limited ability to deal with the Japan that awaits them outside of work, they rely heavily on the bilingual secretaries for everything from problems that arise with their company-sponsored housing to all of the extra, personal duties associated with the stereotypic secretary of industrialized America. Secretaries also take on the role of language translators and cultural interpreters. This role makes the secretaries acutely aware of their EM's dependency upon them, allowing for a type of power that is not available to them when they work for a Japanese manager. Some of the secretaries portrayed their role as one of teacher.

Depending on their personalities, secretaries provide the newly arrived EM with a sense of things in the EM's immediate division as well as the company at large. This introduction is usually the EM's first experience with an employee population that is almost entirely Japanese. The more intrepid among the secretaries will be open with their bosses about the nature of employee reservations concerning the new EM and try to steer the EM clear of mistakes made by predecessors. Secretaries who work for EMs are likely to take stock of the department and the company as a whole, thinking about the big picture in the process, from what they consider to be the managerial perspective.

As to their work relations with EMs, bilingual secretaries had a number of comments, both positive and negative. The positive aspects revolved around respectful treatment of subordinates on a personal level, while the negative focused on an EM's lack of proper regard, a kind of disrespect, for all the work that preceded his arrival in Japan and the knowledge that could be gained from it, particularly in regard to Transco's dealings with Japanese companies. Thus in the intimate realm of superior-subordinate relations secretaries were positive toward Americans, while in the public realm of relations between Transco and Japan, they were negative.

Despite a lack of work experience outside of Transco, secretaries believed that EMs treated them with more respect than would be the case in a native Japanese institution. On this point, secretaries were in complete agreement with women in management. In evaluating the work performed by EMs, however, secretaries were more likely to share the viewpoint of Japanese male management.

During a follow-up interview with one bilingual secretary, W-san, we talked at length about recurring problems with EMs. She had experience with both Asian and Western male managers at the middle and higher ranks of management. When I asked about differences between various managers she has known, she described the American male managers as neither "moderate" nor "considerate" and more dependent upon her for arrangement of what she termed "private tasks" related to their personal lives. Asian managers, according to her, even when they suffer from the same language barrier as an American manager, do not require so much help with their personal lives in Japan. She quantified the ratio of private tasks to company-related work for an American manager as sixty-forty.

What makes the American male manager immoderate and inconsiderate are two main things. First, in delegating both work-related and private tasks to her, American managers tend to make numerous changes to or cancellations of plans, without regard to the consequences, which can be fairly serious in Japan. Unlike the American business culture where people are constantly trying to renegotiate more effective use of their time, in Japan business people expect that a commitment, once made, will be followed through; otherwise the commitment would not have been made in the first place. There is greater sensitivity to business ettiquette and the consequences for ignoring it. Thus W-san found herself having to apologize all the time to the Japanese people with whom she was working to rearrange her manager's schedule outside of the office (one does not need to apologize for constant change within the walls of Transco) and then having to renegotiate schedules with people who were becoming increasingly indignant.

Second, in relation to the management of their particular division at Transco, the common perception among Japanese employees was that American EMs tend to arrive in Japan with an eye for revolutionizing the way things are done without much willingness to learn about the past history of the division. The Japanese employees were likely to attribute this behavior only to Americans.

The thread of the complaint was quite similar from person to person. A male (the examples always were male) EM arrives in Japan knowing that he has a set amount of time in which to make a name for himself in order to be reassigned upward and outward. He has an agenda for change. He begins immediately to implement the new agenda with little or no input from the employees (mostly Japanese) who have been working in the division prior to his arrival. A meeting occurs in which the new division head outlines his reforms and asks for feedback. Little feedback is given because the employees have been through this same scenario every time a new EM arrives (every couple of years), and based on past experience they do not believe that their feedback will make any difference.

What would the feedback consist of? Statements concerning the fact that two or three of the so-called new ideas have been attempted in the past five or ten years with inconsequential or perhaps even detrimental results. In other words, there is a clash between the employees' remembrance of and attitude toward the local institutional history and the new manager's desire to start fresh and establish his role as the new division authority. The new manager does not want to appear lacking in authority and so tries to establish his primacy initially by dispensing his ideas in an atmosphere of limited debate. The employees treat his suggestions with a jaundiced eye, focusing primarily on the ones that remind them of past efforts, and are quick to assume the pattern they see is repeating itself yet again.

I do not wish, by the account given, to undermine the successful operations of Transco. It is, in general, a highly successful company, both in Japan and worldwide. Within the pattern outlined above, however, the manager is undermining both female and male employees, and the employees are undermining the manager. As I have said, eventually this problem is resolved and some measure of trust established between the manager and the employees in the division. It is also true that different managers establish trust sooner than others based on a number of factors, such as his perceived personality, ability, and interest in Japan.

And yet, the frequent rotation of expatriated management in and out of Japan frustrated the Japanese personnel, especially the men, who saw it mainly as further evidence of little regard for continuity. They were aware of the importance of continuity in native Japanese corporations and believed it to be valuable. Management women were likely to mention the general chaos caused by the rotation of EMs, but they never cited traditional Japanese corporate continuity as the ideal. They were more focused on their belief that EMs represented fair treatment to women as a corporate ideal. And bilingual secretaries highlighted the cultural weaknesses of the new manager in terms of his failure to respect both Japanese culture and the experience of the Japanese employees.

When EMs characterized Transco, they tended to feel that the Japan operations were not yet ready to go it alone without the guidance of expatriated management. In fact, Walter, the head of Transco, described the relationship between the senior American management and the Japanese employees as similar to that between parent and child. The Japanese managers were "maturing" but still in an adolescent stage of development. One of the key markers of their adolescence lay in the difference between values as absolutes and values that change based on situation. Walter regarded Americans as absolutist and the Japanese as situational with respect to values.

For Walter this difference prevented the Japanese from having the "vision" necessary to guide Transco. He stated that "values are essential to the creation of vision, but for the Japanese values are situational so vision becomes impossible." Walter believed that individual behavior should be determined by internal values rather than external situations; thus he felt that the Japanese needed a preponderance of rules for behavior to make up for the missing guidance of absolute values.

Partly based on a gender difference among Japanese, Walter also felt that it was easier for Japanese women to come into Transco and adapt to the new environment. Because Japanese women are more clearly looking for an alternative work environment, their expectations are likely to be more in line with the types of values the company hopes to foster. Japanese men, he thought, enter the organization with expectations that are more contrary to company values and they are less adaptable than Japanese women, who unlike Japanese men, "have been doing it (adapting) all their lives."

If Japanese women in management were, in fact, better at fitting into Transco's work environment, they did not seem to be less confused than Japanese men over their role in the organization, and they even seemed to grow more confused than the men as they moved up the corporate ladder. A strong sense of identity often was difficult to discern at the higher levels because the requirements for solid work performance became more opaque.

This opacity promotes uncertainty and dampens trust and commitment even when employees choose to remain with Transco. For all Japanese employees, organizational concepts become more opaque up the line of responsibility, and women face the additional problem of career uncertainty. What does *globalization* actually mean in terms of changes to one's understanding of one's job and career? Even if a manager understands the new requirement to coordinate production and distribution with offices in Europe, how does this requirement affect behavior at the local workplace?

If Abe-san is correct, and the process flows from the top down but without conveyance of shared meaning, Nobu-san's "let's go global!" is the very embodiment of opacity that might lead to homogenous groupings at the highest levels of Transco in order to reassert a sense of trust in one's peers. Thus, in regard to management of personnel, globalization leads to more rather than fewer opportunities for both subjective interpretations of concepts and vague one-on-one evaluations of employees. As senior EMs drove Transco toward some murky idea of globalization, conceptual confusion among the Japanese naturally increased, but more important was the fact that EMs seemed to display an increasing tendency to evaluate the Japanese employees on the basis of both gender and cultural stereotypes. If EMs had placed themselves under the same harsh light, they might have discovered their own sources of confusion and worked to pull everyone together on the same conceptual and evaluative paths. Instead, they operated as if they all understood the same things and avoided any demonstrations of uncertainty.

4 Identity and Perception at Transco: Manifestations of Confusion

G iven that organizations are collections of individuals, the uniqueness, as well as the fluidity, of a given organizational culture stems in part from its particular mix of people at various points in time. Individual employees affect both one another and the organization and, in turn, are affected by the organization as a whole. The dynamic of constant change creates a work environment in which employees must continually negotiate their sense of identity and belonging. The process of fitting in is obvious for new employees, but even longer-term employees have repeatedly to seek their individual fit with the organization. They make impressions on new co-workers, are considered suitable (or not) for new projects at work, have to respond to variations in corporate directives, and have changes occur in their home lives that have an impact on their work lives.

Even without this environment of change, employees are not fully open to unbiased assessments of one another. They enter the organization with preexisting beliefs rooted in cultural constructions that are then applied to the organization. A parallel can be drawn to statistical discrimination theory, which states that in the face of uncertainty, employers utilize societal-level assumptions about categories of people (men versus women, for example) to make decisions about individual hiring and promotion.[1] Similar efforts at "efficiency" of thought exist throughout the corporation, as evidenced by some of the cultural assessments described in Chapters 2 and 3. Even if one were aware of bias, it simply is easier to function on the basis of commonly accepted assumptions than to have to form new impressions constantly, but efforts toward the latter will lead to greater recognition of each individual employee's true potential.

Moreover, people do attempt to influence the thinking of others, even if their own ideas are more reified. The issue is the balance between people's ability to change perceptions others have of them and the generalized assumptions that circumvent new thinking. Within the terrain of Transco, employees' individual efforts at control of their image ran up against ingrained ideas about American versus Japanese culture and female versus male gender. By the same token, Transco's efforts to control employee perceptions of the corporation ran up against similar assumptive blocks, and senior management itself employed this kind of efficiency technique, making sweeping generalizations about the two cultures on a regular basis as one way to assess employees and track the progress of the organization. Gendered thinking was not so out in the open but was quite operant at the level of practice. A great deal of confusion resulted from this array of conflicts.

Statistical discrimination, though in theory motivated solely by the dictates of profit maximization, serves nonetheless to prolong the existence of social discrimination. As such, it becomes a mechanism for self-replication under capitalist reproduction strategy. The dominant group maintains its power by resorting to itself as the safest bet in the face of uncertainty, unless it has a clear reason not to do so, such as hiring Japanese women into management to increase competitiveness in Japan. Once these women are hired, though, the corporation cannot go back to business as usual. New routes to advancement have to be created; self-replication of a senior management archetype becomes a losing battle, and the stakes are higher in the employee mix of the transnational corporation. Avenues to discrimination lie in both culture and gender, but it is questionable whether or not cultural and sexual hierarchies are necessary components of any form of capitalist reproduction.

The focus of this chapter is on a comparison of the individual and organizational manifestations of culture and gender confusion at Transco. The key questions addressed are

1. What sorts of gender and culture confusion arose in this globalizing corporate culture, and how did employees negotiate them?
2. Did preexisting attitudes about gender and culture differences prevent the creation of a corporate culture in which employees were evaluated fairly?

First, I will present a case of gendered perceptions of personality, followed by an example of cross-cultural miscommunication. Second, I will take a theoretical look at constructions of culture and gender in the context of the organization, leading up to Transco's characterization of the ideal employee and the problems, inherent to the image, that emerged both within and between categories of employees, including the expatriated management. Third, I will compare two development programs for Japanese women in management: one successfully encouraged Japanese women to set their own scope for the program, and the other set the scope for them. These programs were designed to expand Japanese women's views of their role as managerial employees at Transco.

Gender Confusion

At the individual level, Erving Goffman (1959) has written extensively on the presentation and representation of self in social interaction, arguing that people go to great lengths to try to control the impressions they give to others, a form of performance he refers to as *dramaturgy*. It is through interaction with others that one's self identity comes into focus. "Individuals work their performance so as to provide others with the materials by which they infer that a creditable self confronts them" (Freidson 1983:359).

These efforts at presentation of self are limited by a lack of control over events both within and beyond the immediate encounter. They are also limited by a lack of control over the precise impression given to the audience. For one thing, audience members may rely upon the "ungovernable aspects" (Goffman 1959:7) of the performance, such as involuntary facial expressions, to formulate their impressions of the performer. For another, there is no guarantee that interpretations of the signs contained within an encounter are the same for all, despite relative consistency of societal norms. Goffman describes an "interactional *modus vivendi*" (1959:9) in which participants agree not on an interpretation of the encounter itself, but rather, on whose interpretation will hold forth for particular elements of the encounter. Transco's hierarchical structure usually means that employees award the privilege of primary interpretation of an encounter to the person holding the highest level of authority, but culture and gender differences among participants can readily thwart both the award and the exercise of that privilege.

Goffman's ideas on dramaturgy leave room for expansion into the terrain of gender and cross-cultural differences in the manner of presentation and in the ability of the performer to control audience perceptions. This expansion demonstrates the resolute nature of gender relations under capitalist reproduction. The construction of gender is based on a "man-woman" binary in which women generally hold second place rather than an equal position in the traditionally male domain of work outside the home. This factor is likely a determinant of not only whose interpretation of a given work encounter receives priority but also the extent of the actor's control over the audience in the face of statistical discrimination.

At Transco, gender factored into employee perceptions of one another's performances on a regular basis. To start with an extreme example, behavior that was deemed outrageous could permanently mark women in a way that it did not mark men. Thus women were more likely to have a difficult time rising above mistakes in presentation, as shown by the case of two Japanese employees, one female and one male, both of whom deviated from accepted (American as well as Japanese) norms in terms of temper.

Ono-san, as mentioned previously, was the highest-ranking woman at Transco, the only one on the bottom rung of senior management, having worked at the company for more than twenty years. In addition to her positive reputation as a very capable employee credited with numerous marketing successes, she developed a negative reputation over the years of having a bad temper. Essentially, she was given to yelling out loud, mostly at subordinates. This subject emerged unsolicited by me in a number of interviews. At first I assumed that awareness of Ono-san's temper was limited to people with whom she had worked directly, but eventually I came to realize that she had achieved notoriety throughout the company.

At the same time, there was a story of a Japanese male employee in middle management who worked in Research and Development for a number of years but had left the company a few years back. His name came up one time as part of a conversation about Ono-san with a female American manager in Human Resources. He reportedly was also ill-tempered but had gone beyond yelling to do things like throwing hot coffee into the face of a secretary, an act far worse than anything I had ever heard about Ono-san, whose temper was limited to the verbal realm. I then took the opportunity to make casual mention of both people to nearly everyone I met at the company, trying to gauge whether they had heard of either of them and the depth of their reaction. Every single person I asked, no matter her or his division, no matter how long or little they had worked at the company, had heard of Ono-san in a negative way, but no one outside of the male employee's original department remembered this man in any particular way at all. And for those within his original department, the mention of his name generated far less reaction.

This example could be dismissed as potentially unfair in the face of Ono-san's continued presence in the company and this man's departure from the scene some years before, but there were other examples of current male behavior comparable to Ono-san's that also evaded permanent association with a negative reputation for personality. Also important points to consider were that Ono-san's division was facing a decline in profit share and that her personality was increasingly viewed by senior management as a causal factor, despite the fact that her behavior had been ignored throughout the time she was inarguably successful on the job. Two Western men in upper management, one American in R&D and one European in Marketing, also had volatile personalities. The former was considered quite capable in his work by most people while the latter was not, but personality was never cited as an explanation in either case. Personality seemed to have nothing to do with assessments of their work.

Yet Ono-san's burden of reputation followed her everywhere, even at the lower levels of the organization. For example, Ono-san was invited at the last minute to an in-house conference on career development. When news of her impending attendance spread, people literally panicked over catering to her presumed "special" needs, including some discussion as to whether or not the lunch menu would be acceptable to her. However, not only did she make no fuss over the food, her participation in the conference was the highlight of the event; and after the speeches were over, it was she that people crowded around for the informal question-and-answer session.

These counter examples of Ono-san's good side never served even to mitigate the negative aspects of her reputation, let alone supersede them. Her good side was always the anomaly. Nor were attempts made to relegate her displays of temper to the limited arenas in which they occurred, training subordinates and fighting for resources. The latter certainly was behavior that male managers engaged in, but there also were men like the two mentioned above who regularly displayed poor emotional control.

One can argue, of course, that control of one's temper is the preferred norm in any organizational setting, but the issue is the extent to which men and women pay different prices for deviation from the norm. Ono-san's temper, though not unnoticed throughout her career at Transco, was largely ignored as long as there was a clear association between her work performance and corporate profit. Once that relationship weakened, senior management seemed to prioritize her personality over any possible external explanations and decided she was no longer suitable for further promotion to positions where she would be working directly with them. The price for deviation is likely higher for women unless they never fail to deliver something that the company wants,[2] thus we have to consider what that higher price may indicate about gender-based differences in attitudes even when the accepted gender norm for workplace be-havior is presented to the Goffmanesque audience.

Drawing upon the results of hundreds of studies conducted from the 1970s through the 1990s, Valian (1999:11) argues for the omnipresence of "gender schemas," that is, "intuitive hypotheses about the behaviors, traits, and preferences of men and women, boys and girls" in all forms of human interaction. These noncon-scious schemas, as Valian describes them, are acquired from early childhood on, show a remarkable similarity across both genders, and serve to oversimplify as well as amplify differences between fe-males and males.

Valian argues that, with the exception of sexual reproduction, the sexes in actuality are much more similar than they are different,[3] yet we essentialize physical differences and exaggerate nonphysical dif-ferences to make sense of the world. It becomes necessary for a *man* to be something quite different from a *woman* to explain logically why men and women operate in different domains. There are gender schemas for *masculine* and *feminine* and all other related terms, and there also are gender schemas for concepts such as *professional* and *homemaker*. Pairings of gender schemas reflect individual and societal patterns of thought; *male executive* and *female homemaker* are more congruent than *female executive* and *male homemaker*.

Relative congruency (or lack thereof) has an impact on the eval-uation of an individual's professional life, with the result that gen-der schemas serve at one and the same time to advantage men and disadvantage women in certain realms of corporate life. Gender schemas may serve to advantage women in female domains such as motherhood or traditional female employment, but such schemas also end up keeping women in their place, providing the emotional support expected of mothers, nurses, flight attendants, and so on, rather than moving women on to the supposedly male professions. Gender schemas no doubt constrain men as well. At the level of the corporate executive, a man boosts his masculinity by being successful in his position, and we do not blame his fail-ures on his gender. By contrast, a woman generally does not boost her femininity by succeeding in her executive position, and when she makes mistakes on the job, her gender often is assumed to be part of the reason. Men are generally thought to be in control of their emotional state even when they provide evidence to the contrary, while women who describe themselves as "hard-boiled" are considered sadly out of touch with their true emotional nature.

Valian's work suggests that Ono-san paid a higher price for negative behavior and also received less reward for positive behavior in terms of being valued as an employee. Though it is true that yelling is not a feminine trait, lack of emotional control is. When our Japanese male threw hot coffee and engaged in his own emotional outbursts, they were treated as isolated events unrelated to his masculinity. By the same token, Ono-san's numerous examples of exemplary behavior were the isolated events, never to overshadow her typically feminine lack of emotional control. For Ono-san then, according to Valian's argument, her numerous professional successes (and they were quite numerous) could not mount up to counter occasions of failure in the same way it might have for a man, and negative traits were stressed to a stronger degree, particularly as she moved up the corporate ladder.

As she moved up in rank, she worked with increasing numbers of men in general and American (white) men in particular. Because I was so often made aware of her temper as a factor preventing continued achievement on her part, I could not help but wonder why she had gotten as far as she had over the years. One reason is that she initially served a pioneering role as a Japanese woman in management at Transco. She had sustained some tolerance of her behavior because of that role, yet even her role as a pioneer was being used in a new way against her. Walter, the current head of Transco, characterized her as similar to the stereotypic American woman in management during the 1970s, whom he described as having "a large chip on her shoulder."

Another reason is that, as a pioneer or not, she delivered profits to the company at a time when such profits were harder to come by, early in the company's time in Japan. It is true that she was responsible for a number of marketing successes; it is also true that she yelled then as well as now, when her success was perhaps less clear. Ono-san was not clearly linked with the success of a particular marketing campaign as she had been in the past.

Her division as a whole was experiencing a decline during my fieldwork, but it was not an exception. Other divisions also were struggling in the difficult Japanese economy of the so-called "lost decade." Though there could have been any number of reasons why the division under her management currently was performing less well than hoped, including reasons that were wholly outside her control, Ono-san was assumed to be a key problem. The current lack of clarity relegated her past successes to the archives of the organization's history and her yelling to the category of intolerable. Gender schemas had existed throughout Ono-san's career at Transco, but suddenly they were being used specifically to make a case against her.

We can also make a case for the increasing power of gender schemas as women in general try to move up the rungs of the corporate ladder. It has been argued that informal criteria based on personal assessments of an individual's character become increasingly important for promotion as one advances in an organization or moves to greater realms of power in business politics as a whole. Uncertainty and the need for trust rise in tandem with levels of responsibility, increasing the incentive to replicate oneself as a means of control when choosing subordinates and voting on prospective members or peers.[4] Since most senior management of organizations and members of elite business politics circles are still men, the propensity to choose other men remains high, and gender schemas may be one reason why males are assessed as more appropriate for promotion. This propensity is confusing to women, especially when they are promoted steadily up the ranks only to face sanctions for the very qualities that took them to the door of senior management in the first place. Negative assessment of Ono-san was not an isolated event; the details of another Japanese woman who had the same experience appears in Chapter 5.

Culture Confusion

Further complexity of variables related to people and identity lies in the respective national cultures dominating the transnational organization. The most salient binary in this regard at Transco is the

American and Japanese national cultures. Each culture is represented and perceived independently, and there are also many opportunities for transection and overlap. In the workplace, "Japanese-ness" transects "American-ness," and vice versa. The permutations of employee types, the opportunities for missed communication, the potential for conflicts, all grow immeasurably as people attempt to negotiate their identities within a decidedly cross-cultural arena. Like gender schemas, culture schemas affected employee interactions.

Cross-cultural settings further complicate the representation and perceptions that form the core of human interaction because impression management becomes subject to these additional, potentially conflicting variables. Of paramount importance are differences in assumptions as to what constitutes social and behavioral norms. A cross-cultural performer makes judgments about appropriate behavior in the other culture in part by drawing from the norms in her or his own culture. These cross-cultural perceptions of and attempts to replicate normative behavior may or may not be regarded as correct by observers of the behavior.

At Transco the dress code allowed for Fridays to become *casual day*. Dressing casually on Fridays is a common feature of American business life, but at least in the more traditional companies, normative behavior still limits the range of acceptable attire on these days. At present the Japanese business context has no similar concept, and partly in response to that, every Friday a sign was placed at the inner entrance to the building, where both employees and visitors had to pass. It announced to visitors that casual dress was in effect for the day, presumably to provide some context for Japanese visitors to understand the visually diverse nature of employee dress. I, myself, wondered what was going on as I rode the elevator from time to time and noticed people's attire—I did not read the explanatory sign until several weeks after my arrival.

The problem was that Japanese employees of Transco also had no set context for understanding appropriate limits to the American concept of *business casual attire*. Although many people opted to wear the same types of business-appropriate clothing they wore on other days, it was not uncommon to see people, younger Japanese men in particular, arrive for work on Friday attired in "dirty-styled" jeans, sneakers, and a ripped tee-shirt. Women who made a conscious attempt to wear something "casual" were more likely to dress in a sexualized manner, with very short skirts or low-cut blouses. Essentially people became caricatures of grunge rock stars, female pop singers, and the like. Casual day was eventually eliminated with little fanfare.

A number of different cultural frames are contained within this example. In dress, the Japanese context is one in which determinations of appropriate attire often are set by people other than the individual, from requirements for school uniforms to company uniforms; dress requirements affect both men and women, but companies often require uniforms for secretaries and even management women on occasion. And in the absence of company uniforms, acceptable workplace clothing still is limited to fewer colors (black, gray, navy blue, tan) and styles.

For women with an interest in fashion, numerous magazines exist in Japan, as they do elsewhere. What marks the Japanese fashion magazine, however, is the manner of instruction on dress, which assumes an authoritative teacher/student relationship between the writer and reader. Articles will provide information on a complete outfit—from the basic clothing to the particular accessories—with an attitude of what *must* be done. For example, purchasing a particular dress might entail the necessity of a certain scarf from a certain store; a specific type and color of handbag; shoes of a single acceptable style, height, and color.[5] In other words, even the greater freedom to dress as part of achieving adulthood often is prescribed. Casual day was defeated by competing prescriptions—the Japanese one highly stylized but "inappropriate," the American one more loosely defined but "appropriate"—and the corporation did not step in to assert its power to define a clear range of acceptable attire.

Transco's choice simply to dismiss the option is telling in and of itself. Particularly in current business organizations in the United States, it is not unusual for employees to receive precise instructions on the meaning of *appropriate casual attire,* including written lists of dos and don'ts handed out to new hires. This remedy was not attempted at Transco, which may be reflective of a negative cultural judgment about the Japanese ability to adapt to American preferences. The source of the confusion was eliminated rather than repaired.

Before we turn to further manifestations of gender and culture confusion at work, it will be helpful to build on both the work of Goffman and the two examples I have presented with further theoretical considerations of culture and gender as social constructs. From there, we will take a look at the organizational culture of Transco in terms of corporate characterizations of the ideal employee. This idealized employee type affected recruitment, hiring, and promotion, in both conscious and subconscious ways, and the (mis)perceptions of ideals is one measure by which employees evaluated themselves and others.

Weaving together characterizations of the ideal employee with a detailing of several layers of interactions as they were observed at Transco, the remainder of this chapter will assess people's perceptions and representations of themselves and others, as well as the challenges both men and women faced when attempting to negotiate the Transco terrain in Japan. The assessment includes the unique challenges faced by women within the corporation, and how they adapted to different sets of demands, expectations, perceptions, and opportunities that often conflicted with one another in the transcultural setting.

Constructions of Culture and Gender

Expanding on the definition of *culture* provided in Chapter 1, an organization's culture also is defined through the vehicle of its manifestations:

> The manifestations of cultures in organizations include formal and informal practices, cultural forms (such as rituals, stories, jargon, humor, and physical arrangements), and content themes. Interpretations of these cultural arrangements vary. The pattern or configuration of interpretations (underlying a matrix of cultural manifestations) constitutes culture. (Martin 1992:37–38)

Culture is thus a framework that includes larger ideological perspectives as well as smaller ideas about common sense, the latter a loose, cultural system in its own right (Geertz 1983), practices, habits, and so on.[6] Within a transnational organization, there are numerous and overlapping patterns of interpretation.

Individuals function within a given organizational culture on the basis of their perceptions and expectations of others, as well as by attempting to structure or influence how they themselves are perceived and what is expected of them. The organization itself functions in a manner similar to Bourdieu's concept of the *social field*, whereby the organization is more than a site of collected human (employee) behaviors. It is the arena within which human presentations and representations occur, and "within which struggles or manoeuvres take place over specific resources or stakes and access to them" (Jenkins [1992] 2002:84). These resources are primarily economic or cultural.

Bourdieu's concept of *habitus*, on the other hand, refers to "an acquired system of generative schemes objectively adjusted to the particular conditions in which it is constituted." He explains that the habitus "engenders all the thoughts, all the perceptions, and all the actions consistent with those conditions, and no others" (Bourdieu 1977:95). Habitus is manifested in the respective American and Japanese cultures.

In the social field represented by Transco, then, American and Japanese "actors" bring together the "dispositions" (Bourdieu 1977) that they have acquired within their respective cultures, and these initial dispositions form the basis of their workplace practices. Practices are generated by both the habitus and the social field; in this case, they were generated by both the two cultures and Transco. The habitus structures dispositions, which are the "cognitive and affective factors: thinking and feeling" (Jenkins 1992:76), and the social field provides the employees with its particular combination of opportunities and constraints.

What is of interest at Transco is the extent to which a hybrid habitus, an American-Japanese cultural combination, is created by virtue of the existence of Transco as a new social field for the actors/employees, and the manner in which both individual disposi-

to legitimate division of the sexes.[8] But also as a social institution, gender is dynamic.[9] As Giddens's (1984) theory of structuration suggests, human practice, by relying on existing social rules and resources, presupposes social structure, but we also need to account for the possibility of change.[10]

In a gendered division of workplace authority, for example, the division is itself a structure that may constrain the positioning of women in the workplace. But possibilities exist for alteration of the structure in ways that could eliminate constraints. If changes in the structure open up new attitudes among women and men about appropriate gender roles in the workplace, to what extent are nonconscious dispositions realigned to augment (or diminish) these changes? At Transco, realignment apparently moved in reverse order, with the effect of dispositions becoming stronger as people moved up the corporate ladder. Gender and culture schemas were strongest when assessments about who would move to senior management were being made, despite what appeared to be greater acceptance of both women and Japanese further down the organization.

Having a dynamic quality, gender interacts with other social institutions, such as the economy, and creates new opportunities for gender-based discrimination and its dismantling at one and the same time. Capitalism's emphasis on profit and the necessity of capitalist reproduction are two issues that underscore the existence of the workplace as a site of gender struggle.[11] Part of women's contribution to profit is their lower wage base; the control and exploitation of women therefore becomes central to capitalist development. But control and exploitation do not have to be the case through all phases of capitalist development, which perhaps can evolve to include the full advancement of women, if gender schemas evolve, too.

The problem, as Connell puts it, is to determine

a convincing connection between the needs of capitalism and what is specific about gender. It is clear enough that if capitalism is to continue, its dominant groups must succeed with some kind of reproduction strategy. But it is not at all obvious that doing this must produce *sexual* hierarchy and oppression. (1987:44)

If sexual hierarchy and oppression are not necessary to capitalist reproduction, then they also should not be necessary to capitalist forms of organization. Transco is a corporation in which there is commitment to the advancement of women; the Japan operations further see women as a source of competitive advantage there. However, women still are not progressing as well as they should be according to senior management's view of them.

It is essential to restate that in the eyes of senior (American) management at Transco, *Japanese nationals of either gender* also are not progressing as well as they should. This belief was repeated to me by a number of people. Analysis of dispositions rooted in national culture is significant in its own right but also helps to point the way to gender-based dispositions. Differences in national cultures were more openly discussed at Transco, while gender differences were not. It is my contention, however, that the processes by which cultural dispositions interfered with assessments of and by Japanese nationals are quite similar to those for gender. Looking at the further organizational manifestations of culture and gender at Transco leads to explanations why this similarity might be the case.

The Ideal Employee

Although characterizations of the ideal employee differed from department to department at Transco, a corporate sense of the ideal was conveyed to employees at large. It is fair to say that understanding the ideal was more pertinent to the work lives of people on a management track; employees in jobs that would not someday lead to management of the company in the overall (a technical track, for example) had more room to stray from the ideal without career penalty. But as will be shown, awareness of the ideal, as well as how it might differ from one's sense of being Japanese, affected a great many people throughout the company.

Nearly everyone who was on a management track was inculcated with a sense of the ideal employee via both corporate training programs and contact with expatriated managers who were assumed to be representative of the ideal by virtue of their sojourn abroad. (Depending upon one's career trajectory at Transco, expatriation was a necessary step for which people on their way up the corporate ladder were "tapped.") Expatriated managers in Japan tended for the most part to be American/Western males, though there were a number of (generally American) females as well, usually in the middle levels of management.

Whether or not these foreign managers actually represented the ideal employee is quite open to question. However, it is accurate to say that they had been considered successful to date and were likely headed for further success. The Japan market also was recognized as a difficult market for the company as a whole; this further promoted the (incorrect) assumption that only the best and brightest were sent there. Thus Japanese employees and newer employees in particular (who had yet to be affected by the comings and goings of multiple expatriated managers) viewed foreign managers as potential models for their own behavior. Such models could serve as either reinforcement of or counterpoint to what was learned in corporate training programs.

In-house training programs, ranging in type from the more concrete (business writing, communication skills) to the more abstract (leadership skills, strategic thinking), were an important part of career development at Transco. New hires participated in required training; for mid-career people, programs were optional but generally well attended nonetheless. Often an employee would be recommended for a particular program by her or his supervisor; it was an expression of faith in the employee's future prospects at Transco that rendered attendance unlikely to be rejected.

The abstract programs provide a clear window on the ideal ("management material") employee, who may be characterized by the following sets of traits. They are divided into "leadership potential" and "management potential." The ideal employee develops both sets of qualities in her or his move up the line to greater realms of responsibility.

Leadership Potential	*Management Potential*
visionary	takes initiative
creative	action-oriented
direct	results-oriented
influential	cooperative (is a team player)
risk-taking	makes the most of opportunities
trustworthy	treats others with respect
fair-minded	gives credit/takes blame

These essential traits have been culled from interviews and brochures as well as training manuals and lectures given in some of the training programs that I attended. The list is not comprehensive in that other traits were important but not to the degree shared by those listed. And certain traits, such as attention to detail, while assessed positively in a department such as Finance, were assessed more neutrally in departments such as Marketing, unless failure to attend to detail resulted in a clear mishap.

While many of the personality and work-style traits are common to organizations and countries in general, it is also true that at least some are strongly associated with American values and masculinized values in particular.[12] Traits such as being direct and taking more risks—products of socialization as well as personality—are two examples. Both of these go against the grain of values set by Japanese culture. Japanese language is noted for its lack of directness; one might argue that ambiguity is a preferred norm in conversation.

Perhaps part and parcel of the fact that uncertainty (as ambiguity) is reflected in speech patterns, Japan ranks as one of the highest (seventh out of fifty-three, with the United States ranked forty-third) in "uncertainty avoidance," which is defined as "the extent to which members of a culture feel threatened by uncertain or unknown situations" (Hofstede 1997:113). Ambiguous meaning is offset by structural predictability. This relationship is in sharp contrast to the United States, where direct communication coincides with relative tolerance for ambiguous structure and a lack of predictability.

Other cross-cultural conflicts can be documented in light of employee practices that reflect work style in organizations. Japanese organizations tend to be process-oriented, while Transco is results-oriented (having consciously moved away from being more pro-cess-oriented during its early years in Japan). Though the majority of Japanese employees come to Transco right from college, these organizational measures have roots in both educational and cultural socialization. Even at Transco, Japanese employees are predisposed to values that downplay many preferred American traits.

Cultural Binaries as Tools for Assessment

In assessing the potential for Japanese employees to fit the person-ality and work style of the ideal employee, dispositions concerning differences between American and Japanese cultures came into play. In an interview with a lower-management American woman working in Human Resources, she characterized the ideal Transco employee this way: "Transco likes a certain kind of person, even as it says it wants diversity. They want someone with a passion for right and wrong in the way things should be done, a strong sense of values as absolutes. There is not a lot of tolerance for the gray." In comparing these traits to Asia as a whole, she went on: "Asian right and wrong is situational; there's a lot of respect for relationship building. There is also slick manipulation of the language, using 'we' when it really means 'I am telling you.'"

These comments bear comparison to similar ones made by se-nior American management. At one point Walter created a chart for me in explanation of the essential differences between the American and Japanese cultures:

American	Japanese
principles	rules
conscience	shame
absolutes	situational
God	no God
religion	no religion
inside	outside

While not necessarily an incorrect assessment of cultural differ-ences, this list nonetheless draws on a simplistic characterization of a "nationalized other" as set against a "nationalized self." Such a binary approach to country-specific culture—they are what we are not—parallels the binaries found in people's formulations of gender-specific traits. What begins perhaps as a reasonable starting point for understanding differences becomes an end unto itself, locking groups, whether national citizens or respective genders, into representations that constrain individual ability as well as desire to deviate from the norm. For example, a Japanese employee might choose to discuss the rules of only a few situations with her or his American superior, but the binary of principles versus rules would lead the superior to readily assume that the employee was driven by rules. Evaluations of one's self and others based on binaries lead to inevitable contradictions. At Transco this was evident in terms of both gender and culture.

The Ideal Employee as Both Self and Other

Awareness of the ideal employee as characterized in training programs and by the existence of expatriated managers as potential models provided one measure by which Japanese employees made evaluations of themselves and their coworkers. Because some people invariably did better than others on any number of traits (relative fluency in English was one marker; a more outgoing personality was another), people sought explanations for their shortcomings. The tendency to seek explanations outside of oneself, although a normal, human reaction, created the potential for conflict.

The type of value judgments that are attached to encounters between employees of different nationalities are complex. In part because people are looking for explanations that will help them achieve operational understanding at work, it is no surprise that thinking becomes rooted in stereotypes about the "cultural other." Value judgments about employees, whether made by senior management or lower-level workers, often are rooted in a nationalistic discourse that can take on a life of its own and, if left unchecked, lead to problems. At Transco, there were problems of perception and sometimes of outright antagonism between American and Japanese but most often between Japanese and Japanese at the lower levels of the organization. (There also were problems between Chinese and Japanese, but the historical legacy between these two nations seemed to be the principle factor.)

Problems between Americans and Japanese were not uncommon, but there were few instances of overt hostility. The former is not surprising given the nature of Transco: an American company in Japan run by mostly American males presiding over a predominantly Japanese workforce. In addition, Transco is a company that sees advantage in being distinctly American in Japan; it was current management's policy not to compete against Japanese companies by trying to outdo them in a Japanese style. Thus the pressure rests upon the Japanese employees to become someone quite different from what they would become in a typically Japanese corporate context. The Americans presumably meet this criterion by virtue of already being Americans.

The reasons for the lack of overt hostility are many. For one thing, everyone had chosen in one way or another (if only by default in cases where one's first choice was removed) to work for an American corporation, in itself a mitigating factor. Of more importance, however, is the fact that the contextual structure of knowledge and expectation dictated that Japanese employees should not only become different but also enthusiastically embrace the challenge of doing so.

As a result, for those who were having difficulty rising to the level of the ideal employee, Japanese hostility toward the Americanness of Transco was rerouted to form a new type of hostility that was intra-Japanese in nature. As a means of criticizing the cross-cultural work environment that privileged American traits, Japanese employees created a new bandwidth of behavior, a reverse polarity with "pure Japanese" at one extreme and "pure American" at the other. Whereas the American management deemed those who were too far toward the Japanese extreme to be unlikely candidates for ultimate promotion to senior management, the Japanese elevated these employees to high status as Japanese nationals. Those who were too far toward the American extreme were more likely to gain the attention of the expatriated management, but could face criticism from their Japanese coworkers as a result.

The Americans also were ranked by the Japanese on a presumed American scale that was, in actuality, extracted as much from Japanese schemas about Americans as from experiences at the workplace. I myself was ranked: people often ventured to give me input as to how I was being received at the company and placed me invariably in a "does not seem like an American" category, which always was intended as a compliment. Factors that were essential to the research—Japanese language skills, quiet presence in the background, extreme efforts to be polite and appreciative at all times, and a desire to listen without offering my own opinions—naturally set me apart from the American employees for whom such characteristics, with the exception of Japanese language skills, would not make for ideal work traits. Even excessive politeness can be detrimental as there were many meetings in which people were expected to represent their views as strongly as possible.

However, there is no doubt that "not seeming like an American" was a good thing in the minds of many Japanese employees. The notion of *pure American* was not a positive one, and American employees who managed, unwittingly, to steer away from this appellation were ranked higher than those who did not manage to do so.

What defines a *pure American* in this context? Japanese employees provided lists of negative American traits that they felt were reflected in the expatriated management. The list is drawn primarily from interviews in which problems were discussed, but also from statements made to me or in my presence at a variety of social situations, both work-related and other.

Negative American Traits
immoderate
inconsiderate
too talkative
too opinionated
does not listen well
cannot speak Japanese
does not understand the real Japan

The term *pure American* is a negative construct whether in reference to an American or a Japanese. The difference is that it marked an American mainly as a point of observation or normal expectation, whereas in reference to a Japanese employee it was intended as a negative sanction in contrast to the *pure Japanese,* who represented all of Japan's positive attributes. These positive attributes were not clearly agreed upon; the saliency rested in the status of the attributes as "not American." An employee could not be both pure Japanese and pure American at the same time. They are polar opposites, whatever their exact characteristics.

Thus a continuum formed between the two ends of the poles, at the center of which lay a narrower band of acceptable accommodation between the two extremes. Exactly what constituted the acceptable range also was unclear; people responded in the negative to people only when they felt the range had been breached. This band functions much like the narrow band said to represent acceptable behavior for women in the workplace, a band contained within the band of acceptable behavior for men, the female range functioning as a subset of the male range.[13]

As a tool for negative sanction, the application of the purity band was similar from case to case. A Japanese might particularly take to American ways at the company, often after returning from a work stint in the United States. However, it could happen just as easily without that stint if a person appeared to blossom at the company into someone who was more outgoing, decisive, and authoritative in work style. Solid ability in English also was a critical factor. He or she becomes very comfortable and capable at work and might start to attract the attention of upper management. At the very least, American managers would find this person easier to engage with, especially when it came to banter.

When this happens, resentment starts to build in the minds of those Japanese coworkers for whom the culture is not quite as attractive or for whom personal recognition seems slow in coming. Because they perceive that they do not possess what their more successful coworker possesses, they start to attribute the relative differences to the purity scale, placing themselves on the positive Japanese end and their coworker on the negative American end. The adoption of the *pure Japanese* label explains their lack of comparative success as a refusal to sell out their own culture. Such a rationale gets these coworkers off the hook from having to try harder or do better at the same time that it sets the more successful coworker, or opponent, as something lesser than themselves on the scale of national culture.

People were not insulted by being called *American* or any such term that reflected American culture directly. The verbal insult was rooted in the company: the opposite of the *pure Japanese* was called a *Trans-toid*. He or she was the "sucker" who had been fully brainwashed by the company into becoming everything the company wanted her or him to become. A *Trans-toid*, by definition, had lost the essence of being Japanese, having strayed beyond the acceptable band of behavior that combined the two cultures into the terrain at the *pure American* end of the binary.

Some of the people I interviewed were aware that they had been labeled *Trans-toids;* for others I guessed that they also might fit the bill but were not aware of their designation. Those who were aware were unhappy about their status, but had no plans to attempt to rectify the situation. They attributed the problem to the other side, and generally speaking they were correct in doing so. The designation was based largely on jealousy over someone else's success, whether real or imagined, but this jealousy operates at the level of the individual. That the word *Trans-toid* quickly caught on and stuck as a label also reflects efforts to rework the power imbalance at Transco. As Becker (2003:661) notes, "what things are called almost always reflects relations of power." From the perspective of some Japanese employees, they destigmatized Japanese culture by stigmatizing American culture in response to the opposite tack that the organization seemed to be taking.[14] Since Sasaki (2004) argues that national identity is not all that salient in Japan during this period, it would seem that conditions at Transco are the primary source of this nationalization of identity.

Of critical importance also is the fact that more women than men seemed to have earned the *Trans-toid* label, while more men than women seemed to apply the label to others. One reason is that Japanese women generally had greater fluency in English than did their male counterparts. They were more likely, for example, to have majored in English in college. Their knowledge of English enabled them to interact more readily with foreign management and created the impression that they were more willing to adapt to the needs of Transco. Related to this is the fact that speaking in English led to greater freedom of expression for women than what was available to women when they spoke Japanese. It was quite common for women to tell me that they preferred English to Japanese. Japanese men, on the other hand, often preferred Japanese and were more likely to complain about the lack of Japanese language skills on the part of expatriated management.

In using English, Japanese men move from a position of more to less communicative power, while the reverse is true for Japanese women. For Japanese men, Japanese language situations generally entitle them to deference from women and confer the natural comfort that accompanies speaking in one's native tongue. For women, the loss of this type of comfort was made up for by the relative gender balance available in spoken English. Japanese language differences based on sex start as early as kindergarten. "Not only are different words and expressions used by boys and girls, but, more insidiously, some of the ways in which boys address girls cannot be used in reverse" (Saso 1990:62). These differences only increase as boys and girls mature into adulthood. Women are expected to be considerably more polite and less direct than men.[15] Thus, there were personal as well as job-related incentives for women to develop their English-language skills, and often these skills made them at least appear to be adapting more readily to an Americanized version of themselves as employees. As we will see later, many of these women did come to feel different about themselves, adopting a personal version of the ideal employee as self, and they extended this sense of, even desire for, difference to their nonwork lives as well.

Adaptations of the Ideal Employee as Self

The fact that designations such as *pure Japanese* and *Trans-toid* existed makes the case that American and Japanese cultures were considered to be oppositional and that perceived loyalty to Japanese culture mattered as a marker of individual representation, even for a non-Japanese, albeit less so. Everyone had to negotiate the binary of American and Japanese cultures, and there were options other than becoming a Trans-toid. Two other common patterns were (1) to try to become just American enough at work to be successful but avoid the Trans-toid label and (2) to adopt one persona for work and another for life outside of work.

In the case of the former pattern, interviews indicate that it was impossible to do this without some permanent change that was detected by friends and family outside of work. Without interviewing those friends and family, it is impossible to conclude the extent to which the person was really different, or whether people tended to exaggerate differences because they knew the person worked for an American company. In all likelihood both factors were at work.

This pattern represents an attempt to unify the self as much as possible without ending up being sanctioned by Japanese coworkers. Awareness of the tension between the two cultures is high relative to Trans-toids, who found American culture quite compatible with their identities and were less likely to change their behavior whether in the workplace or in Japanese society. As a result of being Trans-toids, many of the women in this group sought to renegotiate their personal lives along lines that they considered as more American, such as attempting more equitable relationships with their partners at home.

The latter pattern of dual personas was evident among a variety of Japanese women at Transco, including those in management, but it was particularly common among bilingual secretaries, many of whom work for expatriated managers in a very Americanized setting every day. During interviews bilingual secretaries did not report feelings of being different as children; hence they were not feeling constrained as Japanese women. They chose their line of work to utilize their English language skills, and with one exception, those interviewed told me that they had no interest in moving to the management side.

The adoption of two personas perhaps represents a creative twist on the Japanese conception of the "inside-outside" (*uchi-soto*) binary, in which people differentiate between in-groups, such as family or coworkers, and out-groups, such as people outside one's family or place of employment.[16] Women would come to work where they spoke English and acted in a more direct manner; then, when they left work, they would revert to a more typical Japanese female as defined by the culture. They would become more reserved and less direct; and for some women even the pitch of their voice would rise as they walked out the door of the office building (a particularly high-pitched voice is one marker of quintessential Japanese femininity).

No one claimed to feel disrupted personally by the two-persona style. Nor did they feel they were being disingenuous. It was a strategy that enabled those who adopted it to succeed in the conflicting cultural demands of Americanized work and a more traditional Japanese life outside of work. As such it should be treated differently from conflicts that might arise from a more American ideal of one consistent identity throughout one's personal spheres. This latter point will be dealt with more fully in the next section in which gender-based training programs are reviewed. Though designed to help Japanese women in management, these programs could also augment gender confusion by adding cultural confusion to the mix, that is, by defining gender problems solely within the American cultural context.

Gender and Culture Aspects of Transco's Training Programs

To analyze further the ways in which women are socialized to behave at work, we need to take a look at training and self-development programs. I will focus on two programs specifically for Japanese women, one of which is limited to women in Manufacturing and the other of which is designed for any and all managerial women. Both are programs that originated in the United States and were then transferred to Japan. Because of the contractual agreement I have with Transco not to reveal their strategic secrets, I will not provide a detailed description of these programs, just an analysis of their strengths and weaknesses through the lenses of culture and gender.

Women in Manufacturing

The program for women managers in Manufacturing had a longer history in the United States but was just getting under way in Japan. At the time of my fieldwork Manufacturing organized and held its first full-day seminar, specifically designed to explain the program as it had been presented elsewhere, to determine relative levels of interest in Japan, and to discuss possible adaptations to the Japanese case. I was invited to attend as a participant-observer. The sessions that involved the entire group were in English because the organizers were mainly two American women managers working in Japan who were familiar with the program back home; the smaller breakout sessions were in Japanese, and I was assigned to one of these for the duration of the program.

Unlike the program that will be outlined next, this program was attempting to bridge any cultural gaps between Japan and the United States by genuinely encouraging the Japanese women to determine the directions the program would take and which aspects would receive the most emphasis. The reason was that the American organizers had been in Japan long enough to understand the different situations between the two countries and were interested in helping Japanese women succeed rather than promoting their own personal program. They also had considerable experience as female management oddities in the male-dominated realm of Manufacturing at both Transco and its parent corporation, and so they empathized with the Japanese women over the multiple problems with difference.

A survey was distributed to gauge the relative importance of a number of issues. The five most important to the Japanese women were, in order of votes received: (1) better career planning, (2) the implementation of more work policies that address motherhood (flextime, maternity leave, etc.), (3) the lack of mentors, (4) improvement in the balance between work and home lives, and (5) the specific lack of female role models. Close behind on the motherhood/family side were relocation problems faced by dual-career couples, and child/elder care support systems. Close behind on the mentor/role model side were Transco men's expectations of

Transco women and general Japanese cultural expectations of women.

The Japanese participants were encouraged to take the lead in the discussions of these items, while the American women sat and listened. There were a number of times when things were said that shocked the American women: one in particular concerned the acceptance on the part of the Japanese participants of the Japanese belief that women's bodies are weaker than men's. This discussion revolved around Japanese women's reluctance to give up monthly menstrual leave from work and other benefits based on their gender that were routinely given in native Japanese corporations as required by law. Though the American women clearly disagreed with the dominant sentiment, they left it up to the Japanese women to decide their priorities.

A video was produced to mirror one that had been put out by U.S. headquarters for women with career interests in the company. The latter was biased in favor of women with money, either because of socioeconomic background or because they already had achieved high positions and attendant salaries. In the video, all of the solutions proposed for women's problems with having a "second shift" (Hochschild 1989; Hochschild and Machung 2003), the dual responsibilities of home and work, were centered on hiring others to do the household chores.[17] In Japan there is a dearth of such kinds of assistance and there is limited physical space in people's homes to accommodate live-in help even if it were more common. So the Japanese women at Transco were encouraged to produce their own video that presented Japanese-style solutions to second-shift work. Rather than hiring outside or live-in help, the solutions were much simpler and included things such as the purchase of a small dishwasher to fit into a Japanese kitchen.

Interestingly enough, though a vast improvement over the American video, the response to the Japanese video was still lukewarm. Even with Japanese women listing the things they had done to lessen the stress in their lives, I heard responses similar to the ones from people who had watched the American video: "It just doesn't seem like me at all." Though it is possible to argue that the Japanese women themselves had a collective mindset that saw more limitations than possibilities for improvements in their work lives, the program for women managers in manufacturing was trying consciously to attend to Japanese culture in its creation of the new network.

The General Program for Women in Management

By comparison, the general program for all women in management was a very recent transplant from the parent corporation that gave little attention to cultural distinctions even though it was intended to be highly attentive to difference by its very design. The program originated in the United States in response to a perceived lack of appreciation for and attention to women's diversity, along lines of race as well as personal situation. Its success in the United States quickly resulted in a desire to make the program transnational.

Though the program was not without considerable merit, it exhibited a tendency toward cultural dominance once it moved beyond its American borders. The intention was good, but the cultural patterning demonstrated in the program was decidedly biased in favor of American values, biases that the women who created the program either could not see or would not admit to seeing.

To be fair, Transco's (American) leadership (in Japan) recognized that cultural biases might be inherent to the new program; though it had operated well in the United States, it had very limited testing outside that context. International experience was limited to one European country and Canada; and in the latter case, the program's three female creators admitted (without any embarrassment on their part) to having been taken aback by the language-based (English versus French) hostilities that erupted during the Canadian session. Since even minimal attention to newspaper articles about the separatist movement in Quebec Province, dominant in the press during this time period (late 1990s), should have alerted people to this possibility, there was legitimate cause for concern about the group's ability to translate the program to a Japanese context. It was this type of concern that resulted in my involvement with the program, again as a participant-observer at the request of Transco.

I participated both in the planning sessions for the program and in the program itself as a participant, and it was clear from the beginning that the three founders of the program were uncomfortable with and resented my presence. The Japanese (as well as Walter, the head of Transco), on the other hand, were insistent on having me there, hoping that I might be able to explain any cross-cultural confusion that might arise. Worrying about the possibility for cultural confusion constituted good planning on the part of the Japanese women. They were expecting to have to engage in prolonged discussions about tailoring the program to specific Japanese needs.

Perhaps the motivation was excessive concern for differences between Japan and the United States—the "Japan is unique" phenomenon—but it turned out to be matched by excessive insistence on the part of the founders that similarities vastly outstretched differences. This assessment might, in fact, have been true if the power to define the similarities had not been co-opted solely by the founders.

The founders of the program paid some attention to understanding differences between the two cultures, but they also were heavily invested in proving that the program worked for anyone and everyone around the globe, seemingly as a measure of their own personal success in creating a program that honored women. Thus they appeared more interested in making the Japanese adapt to the program than in adapting the program to the Japanese. Their response to even minimal resistance to certain aspects of the program was the insistence that we just did not yet truly understand the point of the program.

When I was asked by Transco to participate to help the program adapt to Japan and I mostly found myself on the side of the Japanese women concerning any points of contention, hostility was directed toward me. We would explain our rationale for wanting certain changes to the program, but then we would be treated like novices who simply did not yet comprehend the goal. The reaction of the founders to my presence was quite similar to the reaction of the American and European men at a day-long product category meeting described in the next chapter. As an uncontrollable unknown,

I made certain people uncomfortable, especially those higher up in the organization. I could not be clearly placed beneath them in any sort of hierarchy on which they could depend for control of the situation, and they were not sure what power I might have to affect the thinking of other people higher up than they were in the corporation. I am quite sure the program founders would have refused my participation if Transco (in particular, Walter and Ono-san) had not insisted on it.

I regularly experienced having my expertise ignored by the program's three American leaders. I was likely capable of bridging the cultural divide, having both studied Japan for a number of years and lived and worked as an American, subject to all of the latest thinking on self-help and personal development. But the program founders were much more concerned with gaining control over me than with changing the program. It is possible, therefore, that my presence at the planning session made them more resistant to changes in the program than they might have been otherwise. They put what seemed to me to be an inordinate amount of energy into insisting that women the world over had exactly the same problems everywhere; hence they, as creators of a successful program for American women, were ready to lead the women of other countries to victory.

Whether magnified by my presence or not, this response seems symptomatic of cultural dominance in tandem with ignorance about other cultures, reflecting why Transco's parent organization can see itself as global in cultural terms despite the hegemony of its cultural proclivities. Whatever predilections exist for doing things a certain way or for seeing things from a certain perspective, they are rooted in American culture. This same pattern applies to matters of gender and affects how it is both divided and judged.

A gender-based problem with this program was that it insisted upon "freeing" women from the shackles of womanhood by having them embrace very standard definitions of femininity. Rather than questioning whether or not women had to be beautiful, for example, it encouraged women to see themselves as beautiful no matter what they looked like. This approach is not without its strong points, particularly since most women do accept many of the gender differences insisted upon by the dominant culture, but there are serious drawbacks as well.

For one thing, there is backhanded approval of cultural dictates about gender and beauty; women are supposed to have it and care about it while men are not. So the solution is not to deny its importance for women but rather, to redefine feminine beauty.

For another thing, these ideas led quite naturally to a willingness on the part of the American creators of this program to dictate what *femininity* was and how to take control of it. When they did this, they relied exclusively on mainstream American cultural definitions, but they refused to see that, insisting that women were the same everywhere. The most striking example of this predilection was in their insistence that women feel more powerful about themselves as women when they embrace being "sexy." Both the insistence on awareness of one's own sexiness and the precise definition of it were blatantly Americanized, but there was a refusal to see any cultural construction to this type of thinking.

At one dinner during the planning session, the three women founders asked a Japanese woman and me if we regularly "thought about being sexy." We looked at each other and then barely got out a "no" before the three of them simultaneously gasped "Oh, no!" in tones of great sympathy. When I tried to explain that personally I had no interest in being considered sexy on the job, although such things were important to me in certain aspects of my private life, they refused to believe that this choice was one I could consciously make, whether as a feminist or not. Instead they felt sure that I was fooling myself as a woman, sadly unable to relish my own sexiness no matter where I was going or what I was doing. For the Japanese woman, we could not even begin to debate the cultural relativism of such concepts. There was only one door to understanding one's personal sense of sexiness, and these women held the single key.

Participants were repeatedly exhorted to "stretch themselves" to embrace the American concepts being put forth, yet the leadership never returned in kind any attempt at deference to Japanese culture. Two of the three would not even try most of the Japanese food offered, providing excuses for why they themselves could not "stretch" in this way. At one point during the planning session, we all were taken to a very exclusive Japanese restaurant. The Japanese hosts, including Ono-san but not limited to her, were upset that these women would not even try the dishes placed before them. The whole point had been to honor them in a special Japanese way, but the money and effort were wasted and people were insulted. Most of the Japanese, even if they were not particularly offended in a personal way, ended up concluding that these women were "typical Americans" who have to have things their own way. Then the Japanese were expected to turn around and embrace everything about the program without question.

During the actual program, similar problems abounded. As part of a "celebration" of ourselves as women, we paraded in a fashion show wearing our dresses for the big party at the end of the program and drew lots for winning one of two makeovers (to be performed by men) on the last day. The group discussions during the program proceeded based on very Americanized concepts of self-esteem and individualized self-worth. The group was supposed to engage in psychological and emotional work that almost by definition required crying and letting go in front of everyone in order to be considered successful, highly contrary to acceptable behavior in the Japanese context. The facilitators engaged in extensive use of slang and more formal terminology related to both American culture and pop psychology (*gettin' in sync, pumped up, enabler, congruency*, etc.), much of which was left unexplained because the facilitators were not aware of differences in comprehension of English as either spoken words or cultural concepts.

One very problematic feature, related to the facilitators' interest in promoting "personal congruency," was the insistence that one develop a single sense of self to achieve full psychological and emotional balance. The idea of multiple selves contextually situated within one person, quite similar to the idea of multiple levels to one's personal sense of sexiness, was anathema to the American facilitators, a sure sign of trouble. Considerable amounts of time at the seminar were devoted to this topic despite attempts (made by both me and the Japanese) during the planning session to create awareness of cultural differences in this regard.

For the Japanese, the application of different selves to different situations is not a failing but a strength marking the well-developed adult. One's immediate needs are not always most important. There is a desire to evaluate a given situation and then emphasize those aspects of oneself that are most conducive to a positive outcome for that situation. The fact is that Americans regularly engage in this kind of behavior, yet we proceed as if we have a single self to which we must always be true. The *situational* character of Japanese values was supposed to give way to the *absolutist* character of American values.

In other words, despite the benefit of this congruency approach for those women who were, in fact, seeking a single self, all the women who successfully utilize multiple selves as a way to negotiate the multiple cultural settings—working at Transco while being a Japanese living in Japan—were considered in need of repair. Rather than incorporating all women into the Transco family, so to speak, the tables were now turned. The women who had not felt different from the dominant Japanese culture as children and who wished to remain more fully Japanese in a traditional context were the ones more likely to be one (more Americanized) way at work and another (more traditionally Japanese) way outside of work. They had never been particularly unhappy but now felt they ought to be. For those management women who had felt different and somewhat unhappy as children and young adults, they were now marked as successful for having struggled through to a single self.

A number of outbursts occurred during the three-day program (and smaller ones occurred during the planning session as well), with individual women suddenly objecting to the program, declaring it a waste of time and wanting to leave. However, I also must admit that the evaluations of the program written immediately after its conclusion were quite positive. Women, on the whole, felt that the program was worthwhile, though reevaluations of the program one year later were much more critical of its value.[18]

Thus even for a supposedly internationalized women's development program at Transco, American notions of culture and gender dominated. The full extent of this type of domination, which exists at Transco and its parent corporation as a whole, goes largely unrecognized despite the fact that it has some of the most severe repercussions that domination can have. As the next chapter will discuss, with these kinds of assumptive blocks in operation, it becomes difficult for many categories of employees to exercise the level of authority that is appropriate to their position within the company.

5 Authority as Culture and Gender Dominance

Within any groupings of humans, definitions of *appropriate* presentation of self compete against one another. As was argued in Chapter 4, dispositions arise from culture and gender schemas rooted in one's original culture as well as the hybrid culture represented by Transco. People's definitions of themselves and others in their work environment differ, based on a variety of factors, and such differences have an impact on workplace relationships. Mixed messages are inherent to the corporate culture, and the potential for magnification of these mixed messages grows exponentially in a transnational corporate culture.

This chapter explores the ways in which similarly mixed (and negative) gender and culture messages resulted in further constraints to the ability of women and Japanese to compete on an equal footing with males and Americans in the assumption of authority at Transco. Such messages included ideas about language and linguistic style and were transmitted both in general meetings among different categories of employees and in marketing presentations to senior management. They affected both individual and collective efforts to assume authority at different points in time. Though never openly addressed as an issue in the day-to-day working relationships at Transco, ideas about and attitudes toward authority were displayed in nearly every interaction. The question is whether these interactions tended to parallel the subjective assessments made by senior management that favored the authority of American culture and male gender as people tried to move up the promotional ladder. Within the culture and gender confusion at Transco, was there clarity as to who held what authority and when, or was authority confused as well?

Authority is one factor affecting relationships in the work environment. Generally speaking, official workplace authority is of two types: (1) hierarchical position within the company[1] and (2) recognized expertise in the type of work one performs. Although the former type is more objectively understood and accepted by employees, both types are subject to evaluation and contestation based on gender and culture/nationality.

Authority positions also entitle those in them to a certain amount of deference. Analysis of perceptions of a person's entitlement to deference is weakened by the failure to include gender as a relevant category,[2] as research has shown that the attributes of a particular role are not objectively evaluated by others but, rather, have a symbolic significance that is culturally determined.[3] Cultural perceptions of gender differences become one key to understanding workplace authority. When we factor in the existence of high levels of uniformity across countries in comparative evaluations of occupational prestige,[4] it would seem that subordinates must consider both the role and its occupant in evaluating the amount of deference owed to someone in power.

Authority patterns result from "negotiations" between those with and those without power. Patterns that result from interactions between male superiors and female subordinates in the workplace are described as "negotiated deference."[5] Authority patterns between members of the same sex evolve differently; there is less joking, for example, as exists to reduce tension between the sexes, unless tension arises for other reasons.

For women in positions of authority, the ability to express authority is contested on a variety of fronts. Studies of both American[6] and Japanese[7] women reveal the adoption of a "mothering strategy" to demonstrate authority. For the Japanese working woman, this strategy allows for the maintenance of traditional forms of feminine behavior while providing a rationale for respect of the woman's authority. In the United States, such a strategy is more problematic—it can result in the creation of dependency behavior on the part of the woman's subordinates without eliminating their overt acts of defiance toward her.[8] According to employees of Transco who had worked at corporate headquarters in America, males in authority over females also often adopted the role of father figure, something they did not do with male subordinates. This pattern fits our gender schemas in that these "daughters" did not contest the authority of the father figure, but "sons" did contest the authority of the mother figure at Transco.

Authority patterns are one manifestation of organizational culture. Within the majority of corporations, women generally comprise more gender-balanced portions of the lower and middle range of occupations but only an inconsequential portion of the uppermost range. In other words, women still face a glass ceiling along most avenues to ultimate power, where those in authority effect lasting change on the organization under their control. Ultimate authority, it appears, still remains a distinctly male domain.

Exact hierarchies, furthermore, are not always clear in work groups, particularly those found in a matrix-type organization like Transco. Multiple spheres of authority often come together under the rubric of, for example, a product line that involves several divisions, such as Research and Development, Production, Marketing, and Sales, with varying regional responsibilities for each of these (in Transco's case, Japan versus East Asia versus larger global territory). In meetings involving several divisions, it can sometimes be difficult to discern who has the final say over a particular decision. Thus it is within this type of terrain that people's responses to authority take interesting twists and turns along the lines of gender and culture. We will consider authority at meetings in a general way, potential gender and culture aspects of authority, and authority positions in the corporation.

Authority as Communication within Ranks: Stifling Senior Management

In an example from the top level of Transco, thirteen senior executives were required to participate in a regular roundtable, at which time the more abstract issues of corporate vision and strategies to achieve that vision were discussed. This senior roundtable consisted of eight Western (mostly American) men, including Walter, the head of the Japanese organization; four Japanese men; and Ono-san as the sole female. Though five Japanese members were present, three of these (two male, one female) were already experiencing or else were targeted for reversals of fortune.

The two men (one in Human Resources and in his forties, one in Marketing and in his fifties) were considered by Walter to be stuck in "traditional Japanese ways" that represented the opposite direction in which he was trying to take the company. Ono-san (Marketing, forties) was criticized for the same reasons as were many managerial women in 1970s America—she was considered ineffective because of the weight of the "chip" on her shoulder and her inability to take advantage of "female" qualities of leadership.[9] Of the two Japanese men who did not seem to be having problems, neither was on the line for promotion to general management of the company as a whole. One was in charge of legal affairs and hence more in a staff position; the other was in manufacturing.

Besides Walter as the head of Transco, each person was the lead authority figure in her or his respective division. Walter had full authority over all of the Japanese, but the degree of his authority over other (Western) members of the roundtable varied considerably. Two of these men had responsibilities for Transco in Asia as a whole, which conferred upon them an independent status, but they were expected as well to contribute to the prosperity of the Japan operations. The others were responsible only for Japan but had been placed in their positions and in Japan by senior executives at corporate headquarters in the United States. Thus the roundtable comprised members of relatively equal rank with quite varied responsibilities at the top levels of the matrix organization.

Surprisingly, these meetings were noteworthy for their lack of both eventfulness and personality conflicts. They were very quiet meetings in which people made as few waves as possible, going through the necessary motions, but little more. They were marked by general pleasantries and considerable joking to mask the tension. In my observations of numerous meetings between several of these individuals and their subordinates, I never witnessed similar behavior. Despite the differences between them in personality and style that I saw at their own meetings, here they all seemed to act the same.

More than one of the American attendees confided in me that he felt these meetings were "not worth much" precisely because the members did not "butt heads" with one another. This lack of debate appeared to stem from the nature of the meetings themselves, perhaps in tandem with the presence of Walter. But after witnessing countless meetings between Walter and a vast array of employees, it should be noted that he did not appear to be someone with whom one could not disagree. On the contrary, as a leader, he saw himself as being heavily invested in creating a corporate culture that minimized hierarchy and fostered diversity of ideas and input. But, to put one's ideas out there for consideration at the senior roundtable was to risk having both the ideas and oneself evaluated in a climate of considerable uncertainty.

Thus, the very meetings at which the implementation of "corporate vision" might be hammered out were the ones in which little seemed to happen. Instead, people very pleasantly bided their time and refrained from challenging one another even as they behaved as if the meeting mattered (thus displaying Goffman's (1959) idea of the *front*). Most noticeable was the absence of participation on the part of the Japanese males, but everyone participated far less than they did at other meetings I observed. Ono-san, though she spoke more than the Japanese men, also was remarkably quiet, especially in comparison to meetings in which she was the highest-ranking authority. Some, of course, were not equipped to discuss the corporate vision because of the nature of their work at Transco (the legal division is one example), but most were so equipped and also had a strong stake in both the vision and its implementation.

The factors that contributed to this state of affairs seemed initially to be a lack of both structure and purpose. There was no clear task set before the roundtable; the task set by the head of Japan, creating "vision," is a very nebulous one. As such, it requires a type of letting go, brainstorming without regard to consequences. However, no one wanted to risk appearing "foolish" in the company of so many senior executives—there seemed to be discomfort generated by both the lack of clear hierarchy and the murky ideological setting. Attendees did not seem to know how to present a "credible self," similar to issues raised in Chapter 4.

Gideon Kunda (1992) refers to this type of meeting as an "intergroup meeting"—no single line of authority among members who represent different groups and multiple levels of the organization. As is true at Transco, a matrix-type organizational structure necessitates intergroup meetings because projects often are interdependent. But "authority is vaguely defined and often the subject of dispute" (p. 142). Transco's roundtable, however, differed in its marked absence of dispute because there was no clear purpose to the meeting that would directly affect individual work outside of the roundtable. Discussion of ideology, usually "an incidental activity" (p. 153) in work-group meetings (including team, intergroup, and time-out/nonwork meetings for socializing), became the central activity.

Despite the characterization of ideological discussion as incidental to work-group meetings, Kunda contends that it is within such meetings that considerable pressure exists to "express role embracement . . . [by] making oneself visible, creating an impression, and . . . positioning oneself as an agent of the ideology" (p. 153). This pressure occurs because of the nature of work-group meetings, which are considered more "real" than other organizational activities, such as ceremonies. There are stakes to be claimed and opportunities both to judge and be judged by others. People therefore need to be more concerned with their self-presentation and representation than they do at nonwork-group meetings.

These same conditions that encourage role embracement have an opposite effect, too. People need to continue to work together; conflict is healthy only up to a point. Thus role distancing occurs prior to and immediately after meetings (and also during time-out meetings) as a means to mitigate the conflict that occurs during the meeting partly as a result of embracing one's role.

In the case of the roundtable, where ideology was the focal rather than an incidental activity, role embracement and role distancing occurred simultaneously within each individual. People wanted to be "agents" of the ideology, but the ideology was supposed to be created at these meetings; hence it was difficult to know how to demonstrate any kind of expertise. Participants tried to show enthusiasm while they simultaneously refrained from both participating and revealing their true feelings about the meeting's lack of value, given that the proper role to assume seemed unclear. If senior executives can behave this way, it seems likely that similar factors of hierarchy, expertise, and ideological agency dictate employee presentations of self throughout the company.

Authority as Cultural Dominance: Middle Management Contests

At the level of middle management, regular meetings were also held and attended by a group of people with relatively equal positions of authority in Marketing and Market Research. These are two separate divisions, the former being a *line* (where one is on a track to senior management) and the latter a *staff* (where one stays within a particular division and becomes an expert in a certain area) designation. All those in Marketing had similar responsibilities for different product lines in Japan. The meeting generally comprised four Japanese males, three Japanese females, two foreign males (American and Indian), and two foreign females (Australian and Chinese, the latter with considerable Western experience), although there could be some variation depending on the agenda. With the exception of the Indian male, who is older, all fit the profile of middle managers in their thirties.

Simultaneous role embracement and role distancing were also evident at these meetings, but unlike at the senior roundtable, most individuals displayed one or the other rather than both at the same time. In another variation on Kunda's contention that role

embracement is likely to occur in work-group meetings where ideology is an incidental activity, here there was a further qualification
in that those who distanced themselves from their roles seemed to
do so in response to those who strongly embraced their roles of
ideological agency at the meeting. Relatively speaking, people divided themselves along a Japanese/non-Japanese dichotomy. The
foreigners did the majority of the embracing, with the American
male taking the lead, while the Japanese, regardless of gender, did
the majority of distancing.

This pattern of behavior was reflected in both amount and style
of verbal participation in the meeting, which was in English, lending
credence to an Americanized style that would have been circum-
vented had the meeting been in Japanese. Foreigners talked and
tended toward the more casual American style of random exchange,
interruption of people, and limited self-checking (for example, not
being aware that one might be talking too much); while Japanese listened or at least did not speak very much at all. There was one clear
Japanese male exception who was very assertive.[10] There was no exception on the foreign side; all talked with great frequency, especially
the American male, who had an opinion to voice on each and every
item for discussion. I detected no differences based on being in a line
or staff position. All of the foreigners and most of the Japanese were
on the line; a couple of Japanese were in staff positions; thus even the
Japanese who were on the line did not speak much.

The actions of the foreigners did not seem designed to exclude
the Japanese. Rather, the Americanized style of conducting the
meeting left little room for certain kinds of participation. Silences
were treated as voids that must be filled rather than opportunities
for extended thinking. Certain people dominated whether or not
they had something of value to contribute to the immediate discussion. Despite the fact that this meeting had an agenda that placed a
host of different people in charge of different segments, when a
non-Japanese was in charge of a segment, he or she maintained the
floor because the Japanese did not cut in, but when a Japanese was
in charge, the non-Japanese cut in frequently.

Because no titular head was present among the middle managers, authority was at least unconsciously contested by the for-

eigners in terms of dominance and ownership of the meeting. The fact that the task was unclear augmented the competition for authority. The focus of the meeting was nebulous in the same way as the senior roundtable; ideas were bandied about in a quest for some direction the group might take on a variety of issues. But the key difference is that this meeting was not about ideology in and of itself; ideology was incidental to the discussions, which were more concrete in nature. Topics included filling subordinate personnel slots, but the major issue was how to coordinate better communication links between the two divisions present at the meeting. Thus, certain people began to compete over proper understanding of the links necessary and the best methods for implementation of those links, and seemed to lose awareness of cross-cultural (and gender) sensitivity in the process.

Competition for authority took on primarily cultural dimensions, with gender dimensions operating at a distance. Although there was an agenda, discussion of the items quickly took on an Americanized, free-for-all style that favored the non-Japanese, particularly those males who hailed from Western culture. And among the non-Japanese, everyone adhered to this style rather than something different. Additionally, the fact that all meetings of mixed nationality are conducted in English gives an obvious advantage to native English speakers, who can exert control by thinking faster, talking very quickly, and using slang. It thus seemed that both stylistic and linguistic similarity to the dominant culture of Transco's American roots conferred on people additional authority. Native English fluency became a tool for dominance.

In her book on Japanese communication, Maynard (1997) notes that problems can occur during dialog between Americans and Japanese because of the different ways in which conversation is culturally managed, whether the conversation is in English or Japanese. As listeners, Japanese express much more frequent "back channels," brief utterances and head movements that are active responses to the speaker (p. 139), than do Americans. As a result of this type of difference in conversation management, Americans stereotype the Japanese as "too anxious to please or hurry the conversation along" (p. 214), while Japanese regard the relative silence of American listeners as symptomatic of a lack of "warmth and the values of supportiveness and considerateness" (p. 214).

Interestingly, though I did see some evidence of conversational back channels during meetings between Japanese using their native language, I did not see it in meetings of mixed nationality that were conducted in English. I am not sure whether the lack of back channels on the part of the Japanese was evidence of learned cross-cultural behavior or a sign that they were not as vested in the meeting as they could have been. At this middle managers' meeting, it seemed likely to be the latter, as a strategic claim to power.

The Japanese appeared to respond to the foreigners' assumption of authority with relative silence, neither openly contesting it nor submitting to it. They were silenced by the proceedings, but then they turned their silence into a choice that they were making. Silence itself became a form of indirect contestation, a common feature of small-group interaction in Japan,[11] but it appeared to have no effect on the foreigners and perhaps even accelerated their dominance, thus continuing the cycle.

Many of the Japanese seemed to set up a different set of criteria for participation, based on the value of the time the meeting took out of their day relative to other things they could or should have been doing. Not speaking unless they felt their comment was critical to the discussion became a way to move the meeting along so that they could get to something else more important, or at least prevent this meeting from taking up more time than they felt it deserved.

In a later interview, I questioned Abe-san, a regular participant in these meetings, about his feelings toward these types of exchanges in which the expatriated management dominates the discussion. Comparing the current EMs with their recent predecessors, he felt that there was now a dearth of expatriated management who "try to build the team spirit by understanding Japanese culture." And although he was quick to state that this type of discussion dominance was common to most meetings, he qualified how he felt about it:

> But, for me, or Igawa-san, probably we don't regard the balance of the dialog as important. [If] we feel some[one's]

opinion is totally inappropriate, we quickly jump in and start talking about that. [However,] as long as they keep yelling, speaking up, but they tend to say the same things, they try to build on someone's point of view—so long as the subject continues to be the same—Japanese tend not to jump in a lot, because if we jump in, it takes even more time to finish that discussion.

When Abe-san refers to the idea that one "builds on someone's point of view" as a reason for the Japanese *not* to join in, he is reflecting a sentiment common among Japanese at Transco. This sentiment is not unrecognized by at least some of the expatriated management. As one Western woman in middle management, Lisa, said to me, "The Japanese hate it when the *gaijin* (foreigners) say, 'To build on that point'; one (Japanese) person can speak for the group." However, despite the fact that Lisa appeared to be one of the most effective *gaijin* communicators I observed in more productive meetings at Transco, she, too, fell into step with the dominating style seen at the middle managers' meetings she attended. (An example of a productive meeting is presented in the following section of this chapter.) In meetings that included her subordinates, Lisa used her authority to set quite a different tone, one that included attention to language differences, while at the middle managers' meeting she just seemed to go along with the cultural (and gender) split in dominance.

In the American cultural context is a tendency to feel that everyone must have her or his individual say. While this style has the potential advantage of bringing forth new ideas, it also encourages people to speak even if their viewpoint has already been adequately represented. The Japanese are more apt to let one person represent common sentiment; not everyone has to be individually recognized. Although more efficient in certain ways, this style may prevent people from admitting to contradictory thinking or sudden ideas.

Other cultural comparisons made by both Americans and Japanese about meetings were similar. Americans tended to recognize that they did more than their share of the talking at meetings, but emphasized the fact that the Japanese did not talk enough, while the Japanese did the reverse. One senior Japanese male manager, however, put the blame equally on both sides, noting that "Americans don't understand that fifty percent of communication is listening; Japanese don't understand that fifty percent of communication is speaking."

The "team spirit" that Abe-san mentions also is a concept rooted in cultural relativism. In the more stereotypic Japanese version of *team spirit,* there is considerable attention to the process by which members participate, process being as important as outcome. It can extend even to consideration of the fair allotment of time to speak based on the number of members. In a story that was related to me secondhand, when one Japanese employee of Transco was asked why he had not provided more input at a particular meeting, his response was that the meeting was slated to be an hour long and was composed of ten people; hence each person's maximum share of time to talk was six minutes. It was not that people should use their share; such calculations were an instrument for self-checking, that is, setting the upper limits for each person's verbal participation so they would not dominate the meeting unfairly.

No doubt many Japanese and American meetings, based on either the status of the members present or the particular agenda, carry the expectation that certain people should and will be doing most of the talking, but in the Japanese case there is still greater concern for the attendees as a whole. *Team spirit* in the American stereotype generally is not subject to similar considerations. Though there may be negative evaluation of those who talk too much, achievement of a goal is more important than the process relative to the Japanese norm.

Beyond the advantages of native English language skills and cultural differences in style of participation is a further issue of relative expertise in a given topic for discussion at a meeting. In the case of both the senior roundtable and the middle managers' meeting, levels of expertise were not easily understood by participants because of the nebulous nature of the meetings' content. In both cases, people who had, by prearrangement, specific reports to give, did so with both clarity and brevity. This style was particularly true of the Japanese, who tended to prepare for their parts in a more formal way, while the Americans leaned toward more informal presentations. Japanese tended in general to be more comfortable with scripted participation that they could fully prepare for in advance of meetings. Beyond any cultural preference for this style of presentation, it also lessened the impact of variations in language ability.

However, without the presumption of differences in expertise that would then determine who had a "right" to speak more at length on a particular topic, these two meetings, along with others that I observed, became jumbled and less productive in appearance than meetings in which both roles and tasks were clear. When the discussion opened up after a report, the members of the senior roundtable returned to a combination of a few "safe" comments, made mostly by the non-Japanese, and awkward silences that were relieved by good-natured joking. No one knew how to represent herself or himself as an agent of the corporate ideology. At the middle managers' meeting, the completion of a report always saw the return to a free-form discussion mostly dominated by the non-Japanese who positioned themselves as ideologically superior in terms of presumed corporate expectations regarding style, a view that was encouraged by the use of English as the required language medium.

The senior roundtable, though it was similar to the middle managers' meeting in terms of its cultural mix, was also stifled by the lack of hierarchy, while the lack of hierarchy in the middle managers' meeting resulted in cultural contestation. People with a more Western orientation essentially hijacked this meeting by creating a culture that favored their style of participation. They were demonstrating their value as career managers by performing their jobs along the lines set by Transco culture. The Japanese would have to transform themselves culturally along very steep lines to compete in a similar manner. Unless or until they do, many opt instead to redefine the meaning of such value.

Being silenced, even partially, is a critical issue in corporate life. If the goal of a corporation is to foster original thinking and creative output as one way to stay ahead of the competition, minimizing the contributions of employees who are not patterned on the dominant gender and culture mold is detrimental. That the Japanese are silenced even when the discussion is about Japan is all the more problematic; and later we will see that women could be ignored (another form of silencing) even when their expertise as women was recognized to be of benefit to the particular issue at hand—they were given the floor, but then no one necessarily bothered to listen.

The extensive power of certain forces to come together and restrict people's individual participation is seen in the senior roundtable. This group comprised high-ranking individuals whose capabilities and successes, at least for the Americans, were unquestioned. Yet the lack of hierarchy through which one might have known *when* to participate, coupled with the lack of clear ideology through which one might have known *how* to participate, was able to stifle the contributions of even this group. The roundtable also provides evidence of the power these individuals have in terms of hierarchical rank. If they can silence one another, all the more can they stifle their subordinates, without necessarily being able to recognize the dynamic. Especially if the subordinate is either a women or a Japanese, it might be easier to operate on the basis of generalized assumptions about these categories (women and Japanese are quiet, for example), the same sort of statistical discrimination raised in Chapter 4, than to tackle the roles played by the people in power.

Gender versus Culture in Communication of Authority

Within an organization like Transco, one important difference between the larger categories of "Japanese" and "women" as culture and gender factors for negotiation is that the company ultimately will reward Japanese for becoming Americanized, but will not reward and will perhaps even punish women for becoming masculinized. Becoming Americanized creates the impression that one has joined the ranks; the EMs felt more comfortable with these employees because they were recognized more as one of the EMs' "own." This recognition is simply not possible for masculinized women, who would move even further away from any status as one of the EM's own by virtue of this gender transgression. The reward for cultural transformation appears palpable, but any gender-based rewards remain confused at best.

Managerial women have less overt difficulty negotiating the cultural transformation in part, as related in Chapter 3, because many of them already felt at odds with certain aspects of Japanese culture as far back as their childhood days. Yet most of the perceived cultural discrepancies had and have to do with gender. What they feel is being offered to them at Transco is an opportunity to go beyond the gender barriers maintained in Japanese culture, but then they must go on to negotiate the gender barriers set up in the American context. As the management level rises, these differences are increasingly ones of nuance—how to be assertive without displaying aggression, how to lead without appearing too authoritarian—nuances that carry greater gender and culture limitations for women, with differences that depend on the national culture in question as well as the culture of the work environment.

Authority is a function of gender in part because many of the qualities traditionally perceived to be necessary to authority are considered as inherently masculine. In the case of Transco, authority also was vested in displays of American cultural traits. These gender and culture formulations, so to speak, have evolved into an overall sense of female authority as something fundamentally different from male authority, and of American authority as different from Japanese authority.

For women who tread the waters of masculine-defined authority, there are sanctions. At Transco, I was not made aware of any men who had been told to act more masculine as a method of dealing with authority problems, but I was made aware of women being told to act more feminine.

To return to Ono-san, who was previously regarded as highly successful and promoted up the line over the years but was now considered problematic and an unlikely candidate for further promotion or continued employment with Transco, senior male management had advised her to act more in line with her gender as a better way to cope with her authority. In a conversation about her management style, she related one exchange with her regional (East Asia) superior (an American male):

> In fact, (he) told me that "Ono-san, you are a leader, you have to . . . exploit being a woman in order to become a leader" and I was listening to this and I said, "What the heck is he talking about?" You see, "women are more empathetic," and I'm saying to myself, I'm not; I'm as empathetic as the average man. Women have (something like) intuition. I *do* have that and I use it in Marketing, but I don't know if I should use that more often. I was surprised. I like this (man) very much and respect him, but then it was one major surprise; in fact, the only surprise I heard from him is telling me, asking me, to become a more effective manager, uh, leader, by being more womanlike. I'm a hard. . . . , probably hard-boiled, at least on the job, but I still tried to think this through. But I still don't understand—I do understand, but I don't know what kind of actions I need to take (that would) reflect his comments. At best, I hope I don't have to do like he says in order to be successful, more successful, later. He surprised me because I think there is opportunity for him to better understand me.

In this exchange are two issues of critical importance. One is the obvious (and unfair) assumption that leadership *should be different* on the basis of gender. Second, even if we were to agree that leadership is, in fact, a naturally gendered phenomenon, what does being told to act more like a woman actually mean? And why is it used more often in the case of "problematic" women like Ono-san? She was having difficulties as she moved up to the highest levels of the organization, but it was men who assumed that her gender was a factor. Women who spoke of Ono-san's temperament never mentioned her gender, neither as the explanation for her temperament nor as a reason to see the problem in a more acute way.

Ono-san's case bears comparison to similar trends in American business. In California, a new coaching program for top women executives was highlighted by the media in the early 2000s. Avoiding even the appearance of euphemism, the program was entitled Bully Broads, and was founded by a woman consultant named Jean Hollands,[12] further evidence, along with other women's development programs, of the fact that women can accept these gendered categories of leadership and attempt to teach other women how to remain within the acceptable boundaries.

As one participant said, "I came here—excuse me, I was sent here—two years ago because of my intolerance for incompetence, and for having a level of passion for my job that scared people to death" (Banerjee 2001:C1). The article continues:

> By many measures, these women would seem to need little help. They are experienced executives who have pushed their companies to higher profits and wooed the most clients. But nearly all have been told that the toughness that made them six-figure successes has become a liability, preventing them from rising higher. Their no-nonsense ways intimidate subordinates, colleagues and, quite often, their bosses, who are almost invariably men.

Ono-san's story is remarkably similar. She is a woman who significantly improved Transco's profit base in Japan at a time when it was struggling to make gains. Her personality fit the profile of a "Bully Broad" for most of her career, but was ignored as a problem needing unequivocal rectification until she reached the bottom rung of senior management, at which point it became the critical factor in negative assessment of her suitability for further promotion.

A couple of years behind Ono-san was another Japanese woman who had also moved rapidly up the ranks and was regarded highly, the K-san mentioned in Chapter 3 as previously wanting to be a man to have better career opportunities in Japan. She was sent to the United States as further investment in a long-term career, but after she returned to Japan to resume work in upper-middle management, she, too, started to be regarded by senior American male management as problematic, again based mostly on a presumed masculinity as a key component of her "unsuitability." Unlike Ono-san, she did not have a record of yelling at people, but she had a strong personality and was aggressively intent on a career path that would take her to the senior levels of management.

Gendered leadership was inadvertently defined in another way at Transco. A copy of a memo about a new position was shared with me by some of the Japanese women in management. It had been circulated among all the product division heads secondhand, asking for their input because the original recipient of the memo did not have his own suggestion in mind. The memo was a request for the names of potential in-house candidates to fill a new upper-middle, managerial position in Marketing that entailed consider-able contact with outside advertising agencies and the media industry in Japan.

The memo was asking for someone with "proven strategic thinking skills and the personality to lead/influence" the outside agencies. The selling points offered to someone who might con-sider taking the job were the unusually large budget that one would control, the opportunity to wield "thought leadership" at large, and the possibility for further promotion. At the end of the memo was written: "Incidentally, we prefer to have a male person for this job."

There is little doubt that a male would be less threatening to the Japanese who work for the media and advertising industry in Japan, where men well dominate the numbers of management em-ployees. Yet the Japanese agencies that regularly dealt with Transco were quite used to dealing with women, and Transco was known for challenging gender barriers in Japan. It would appear, however, that these challenges have yet to allow Japanese women to pene-trate the realm of ultimate authority.

However, in an oblique way, Japanese men must negotiate gen-der, too. In my observations of meetings where Americans were in the minority, Japanese of both genders seemed to demonstrate more effective communication skills than the American men did when they were in the majority. The essence of such skills, though feminized (as empathy and generally greater concern for others) in the American cultural context, is rooted in Japanese culture at large. It is therefore a bit ironic that some global studies of national cultures consider Japan highly masculine in comparison to other cultures, including the United States.[13]

During meetings at Transco, Japanese of both genders, even including Ono-san, displayed communication skills that might be considered more feminine to Americans. For example, meetings that I viewed as quite productive, at least in terms of full participation and the exchange of clearly understood information, exhibited far greater sensitivity to people's differences. These tended to be meetings in which there were more Japanese members, lacking a critical mass of Americans/*gaijin*, for example, who might fall back on their own cultural proclivities toward domination by virtue of style.

The participants at one meeting I observed came from Marketing and Research and Development (mostly from the latter), plus two participants from other foreign operations. The discussion revolved around a single theme of global coordination of a certain product line. Participants were mostly Japanese: two men in leadership positions and four women in their twenties and in entry-level management. The titular head was S-san, a man in his fifties who worked in Research and Development. The other Japanese male was Nobu-san, also from R&D. S-san is Nobu-san's direct superior. Also included were three *gaijin*: Lisa, a mid-level marketing manager mentioned earlier in this chapter; a young Australian male present only as an observer for purposes of information exchange with his work at a location outside of Japan; and an English woman (perhaps mid-forties) from a division in the United Kingdom, visiting Japan to help coordinate the global project.

S-san, whom I would describe as mild-mannered and kind, may be the one who set the tone of this meeting, but everyone in attendance appeared to fall reflexively in line with a tone that attentively embraced each and every member. I know that S-san was aware of the importance of sensitivity to other people and thought about his own role in promoting such things. In an interview with him, he told me that he feels he can read his employees better, including their facial expressions, when the meetings are conducted in Japanese, but "to be fair, even one *gaijin* at a meeting creates a necessity for English." He also stated that he tries to pay attention to the comfort level of non-Japanese at meetings even when they are in English.

In terms of language issues, S-san expounded on some of the problems for Japanese employees. For more subtle topics, he said, "those that are organizational or have to do with organizational development where there are so many gray areas," the dominance of English language severely limits the comprehension capability of native Japanese speakers. Some Japanese may prefer English for technical topics, but it is within the gray areas of corporate life and work that language barriers arise.

However, according to S-san, it is difficult to expect any change in the status quo; "even foreigners who stay for five to ten years don't learn Japanese." Thus, pressure to use English comes from the expatriated management. "They demand everyone speak English because this is an American company." This demand is made, despite the fact that corporate headquarters in the United States insists the corporation is (becoming) a global one in many more ways than mere physical location.

Although this meeting run by S-san perhaps seemed more diffused with Japanese culture, productive meetings such as this one were also marked simply by greater awareness of the mixed foreign environment in which people were operating, no matter the national origin of the leader(s) of the meeting. Each member was taken into account, both as a listener and as a speaker, so when the meetings were in English someone usually took care, like they did here, to see that each person was grasping the dialogue, without creating embarrassment for people with lesser language ability. People often were asked if they would like to provide individual input, and if they were newer to English as a second language, the discussion took on a question-and-answer format designed to help them say what they were thinking.

Japanese culture, as such, contributed to productive meetings by the greater concern for and ability to engage in teamwork, but the sensitivity to people's differences was induced as much by the fact that the Japanese were the ones most likely to have prior experience with the feeling of being lost at a meeting, that is, working in a second language that they were still struggling to comprehend. For foreigners who had this experience, they, too, became more sensitive. Lisa, for example, reported to me that when she was a newcomer to Japan she was often at meetings with all Japanese people, encouraging them to mix their native language together with their more limited English-language skills, though her own proficiency in Japanese was quite low. She described herself in those meetings as "always thirty to forty seconds behind, smart but unable to contribute to the fullest," and went on to say:

> Senior managers don't have to experience the frustration and difficulty; there's a sensitivity that comes out of such an experience. Slang has to be eliminated, and people need to slow down. Everything is in the (Japanese) person's mind— what they want, what they need—but they can't get it out. One strategy is to just keep asking questions and it will come out. The teamwork of the Japanese is very helpful.

Cross-culturally, at meetings in which their own cultural numbers dominated, it seems that the Japanese took on the more presumed (stereotypic) traits of female behavior, even when they were male, while the Americans exhibited (stereotypically) masculine traits even when they were female. When their numbers were significant, Americans in particular and Westerners in general dominated discussions, were very assertive, and appeared to have little regard for soliciting others' opinions or sensitivity to their own cultural advantages. The Japanese were silenced by these meetings and developed a different set of evaluative criteria for judging their lesser participation.

When the Japanese were in control numerically at a meeting, they displayed more "feminine" concern for everyone's well-being and the ability both to participate in and to absorb the proceedings. Foreigners who participated in these kinds of meetings fell in step with and in many cases helped to augment the Japanese style. This behavior was especially true if they were women (Lisa being one prime example), but it is important to note that there were, in fact, American male managers whose style was quite conducive to full-member participation. Walter was one, and there were two others in general marketing management.

The problem was those American males at Transco who could not be attentive to such matters. Simple communication was much more effective when the Japanese/female style prevailed, and less effective when the American/male style prevailed. But the latter style was not recognized to be problematic, much less penalized, even when the division attached to the male was not performing up to par. This difference is crucial in comparing the case of Ono-san, for whom style became an issue when her division started to lose market share, and in her case poor style became attached to her female gender.

Within cultures or nationalities, a similar pattern of participatory dominance exists for gender that gives preexisting advantage to males. In the American context, a free-for-all style favors males because participation requires a kind of assertiveness that men are socialized to have in larger measure. Men also are socialized to talk more frequently, talk longer, have opinions with or without expertise, and to take charge. Although socialization is a subject of much debate, numerous studies indicate that this type of socialization begins at home and continues throughout schooling.[14] Women are socialized not to have these traits and thus are more likely to be penalized for displaying them. Women, for example, would be regarded as dominating the discussion sooner than men would under similar circumstances. These circumstances help to silence women; like the Japanese at cross-cultural meetings in which Westerners dominate, there are too many things to overcome—it's easier to acquiesce and maintain a private set of alternative criteria for evaluation of oneself and others.

An Example of Female Expertise Ignored and Male Authority Gone Awry

Authority as recognized expertise is one area in which gender and culture difficulties can potentially be overcome, but the value of the expertise has to be acknowledged on its own, separate from the gender and culture of the person possessing it. Although women were able to consider themselves experts in a particular area of work, it was not necessarily the case that their expertise made a difference in how they were treated in intergroup meetings.

Methods for establishing one's authority at Transco meetings occur within the overlap between organizational culture and the national culture represented by the attendees. This occurrence could be seen vividly in meetings based on a large mix of the matrix organization, where people from numerous areas and levels were brought together. A particular example is a daylong meeting about a single product category, composed of those responsible for Japan and those responsible for Asia as a whole. Most of the full-day participants, all middle- and upper-level employees, were from the main Japan office, but a few were flown in from elsewhere in Asia. Considerable time will be spent on this meeting because it is a good example of how and why certain categories of people can gain advantage over others at Transco.

The purpose of the session was twofold: (1) to exchange information, including the nuts-and-bolts of physical product development and consumer preferences, and (2) to plot big-picture strategy. In attendance all day were six Western males (five American and one European), three Asian males (Japanese, South Asian, and Southeast Asian), and four Asian females (two Japanese—including Ono-san, one Chinese, and one Southeast Asian). The European, Hans, was the regional head of this product category. He normally worked elsewhere in East Asia but had subordinates and one superior in Japan.

This meeting stood out in stark comparison to most that I attended. My presence caused a bit of an uproar, both initially and for most of the morning session. When I walked in with Ono-san, Hans did not believe that I was being allowed to attend the meeting. He took it upon himself to leave and personally converse with his boss, the regional head of East Asia. Since he was the same man who had, in fact, given me permission to attend, rather than Walter to whom Hans was not subordinate (and with whom an antagonistic relationship existed), Hans returned and "allowed" me to stay.

Throughout the first part of the morning, Hans and two of the American men made visual contact with me, and either spoke directly to me or about me to one another. These three men, along with one other American male as a distant fourth, also were by far the most dominant at the meeting over the course of the day. By that time in my fieldwork, I had attended countless meetings, and not once had my presence caused a similar response. In most cases, I seemed to fade from people's consciousness within ten minutes; a couple of times I was asked for my opinion as a consumer when it suddenly occurred to people that I was sitting there in an opportunistic way. This meeting was different somehow, and the three men dealt with their discomfort over my presence by making quite a few jokes. This response was very similar to the joking found in the senior roundtable, but the roundtable was masking discomfort with the topic and lack of hierarchy rather than my presence, as evidenced by the fact that attendees complained to me that the meetings generally were too timid in tone to be worth much.

That these three men, indeed all of the American men in attendance at the product category meeting, were among the most senior at the meeting is a likely factor explaining their behavior. It seemed that, at least initially, I posed a threat to their assumption of full authority at the meeting. They suddenly felt subjected to something and someone beyond their control; they were not sure what "power" I might have as an observer. This contact was the first I had had with both Hans and one of the three leading men; the others knew about me and my research. One worked in Marketing where I spent a lot of time, and I had attended a meeting run by him in preparation for this meeting. The other headed a division from which I had drawn two of my six primary subjects. Neither seemed personally disrupted by my presence in the same way as the other two; it was more that they were brought into and felt obliged to go along with the response of Hans, because they were supposed to be "one of them."

Two people who worked closely with Hans thought it was important to warn me that Hans was a "control freak." I knew in advance that he might object to my presence, but after his discussion with his boss, he felt compelled to go along. However, the issue of Hans being labeled a control freak is central to my analysis of this meeting quite apart from my attendance.

Although the daylong meeting bore resemblance to the middle managers' meeting detailed earlier in this chapter, where the foreigners largely dominated and the Japanese were quiet, it exemplified that characterization to the extreme. My presence appeared to stifle them initially, but within the first hour, the meeting descended into a contest among the American males, in particular the two just mentioned as joking about my presence, for the attention and approval of Hans, the leader on the occupational hierarchy. Everything and everyone else seemed to get lost in the shuffle.

The two competed back and forth, each one speaking at great length whenever he got the floor. Hans, for his part, allowed them to do this without any hint of control, even when they appeared antagonistic toward one another. Several times the antagonism between them resulted in a tension that filled the room and made people uncomfortable, including me.

Hans also talked a great deal, setting the tone and trying to get people to think about "strategy" as his main concern. Indeed, it was strategic thinking that the two men tried so hard to display. The other participants were quiet, save for regular comments made by other American men in attendance and a few comments, but mostly just questions seeking clarification, made by women.

When smaller groups of two or three people came in the room to make a presentation for a particular section of the agenda, these same men consistently failed to pay attention, particularly the one who emerged as the most verbally dominant. He read his own notes and wrote things down that clearly were the result of his own separate thoughts rather than the result of things he learned from the presentations. If there were visuals used in the presentations, he barely looked at them. None of it seemed of interest to him, even though the entire day was supposed to be about exchanging information and putting everyone on the same track for the future, that is, coordinating the needs of both the Japanese and the Asian regional offices.

The only person that Hans consistently corrected and seemed intent on controlling was Ono-san, the sole female there with an authority level similar to the American men. I found myself becoming sympathetic with her because, despite the fact that I was

aware these two had a history of a somewhat antagonistic relationship, Ono-san could not seem to win no matter what she said or
how she said it. On more than one occasion, Hans told her to think
"outside of the box," and though I could tell she was angry, she
was determined not to engage him in any prolonged disputes (she
went into the meeting with this attitude in mind). Ono-san herself
had a long history of thinking "outside of the box." This ability had
been one of the keys to her success in the company.

There also seemed to be a consistent pattern of American men
collectively correcting both individual women and non-American
men who ventured forth with an idea or opinion, but not American men collectively correcting individual American men. If these
men were competing for the approval of Hans, they disagreed
with one another as individuals, but several men often fell together
in line to correct individual women on those occasions when
women's comments were not being glossed over.

One woman inserted some comments into the discussion, and
Hans responded by turning to one of the American men and asking him an unrelated question instead. Later she asserted herself
again and several of the men told her she was right from a "strategic step" but wrong from an "action step." The Indian male spoke
at this time, and they also disagreed with him in terms of his timing
in the discussion, but asked him to hold the thought for some future discussion. (Since I had to leave the session to attend another
meeting later in the day, I am not sure if the discussion ever returned to the point the Indian man was trying to make.) This sort
of dynamic occurred over and over. The exchanges always were
polite and respectful on the surface, but the undertones were clear
nonetheless.

To separate what might have been the result of authority based
on hierarchical rank in the company from that which might have
been related to nationality and gender, we will turn to those cases
where women were, in fact, given more of their fair due. These always were cases in which being a woman created the possibility for
a certain type of expertise the men could not have. Transco's product line extends to both household and personal products used far
more or exclusively by women, and this area was one in which the

woman's point of view was likely to go uncontested. The problem is that these cases were also the ones in which the men in leadership paid the least attention; they did not contest the women because the topic was less important to them, and the women had no authority to oblige them to be engaged.[15]

If a report was being given on test market results for Japanese female consumers, for example, the room became very quiet and the atmosphere appeared respectful. But when I looked around to observe people one by one, three of the American men were not listening at all, and Hans himself alternated between paying attention and doing something else such that he probably gave the report half his attention time. The conversation that flowed after the report was generated almost entirely by the women, and in my opinion contained skillful nuances that were important to everyone's understanding, but the men continued to ignore it all the same.

By virtue of their seniority, these men were more in charge of "strategy," so it is fair to expect them to talk more during those sessions. On the other hand, everyone else also was supposed to be playing at least a smaller role in defining the strategy (let alone learning how to "do" strategy)—that was one of the purposes of the meeting—but their opinions generally were dismissed or contested. Their opinions did count when the subject matter related to femaleness or Japanese-ness as a source of expertise, but the three American men tended to fade out of these subjects entirely of their own volition even though understanding these subjects was directly linked to the strategic decisions that needed to be made. Along with Hans, the American men owned the meeting from start to finish; everyone had to submit to the value of their expertise, but they did not have to return in kind.

The dynamic of the meeting was fully defined in ways that benefited the American men the most. Hans, despite being characterized as overly concerned with control, made no effort to control these men as either speakers or listeners; he seemed to assume that they were naturally on his same page, that they all already were of one mind. Since it was two of the more senior American men who told me that Hans liked to be in control at all times, I assume that he displayed this tendency in smaller meetings just with them, taking excessive control over even them in certain settings where he needed to establish himself as "the boss" in a group of two or three.

However, in the larger mixed setting he established his authority by placing these same men on his side of things, as the locus around which other people's participation was defined, relegating both women and non-Westerners to the periphery. Furthermore, by virtue of his own limited attention to the women and the Japanese/Asians in attendance, he sent a message to those present that it was quite acceptable to ignore certain participants.

Ono-san was in large measure considered "uppity" because she resisted being ignored along these lines. She considered it part of her job to get her ideas out there and to defend the interests of the Japan offices at meetings with global agendas. This sort of "Japan versus global" conflict was common throughout the organization at the time this research was conducted, but Ono-san was penalized more than men were for engaging in it. In contrast to his attitude toward the American males, Hans assumed that he and Ono-san were never on the same page, even when it appeared, to me at least, that they were. By making her a priori into a generally agreed upon "problem" with no cure, Hans and the others did not have to consider whether her ideas had merit or whether they themselves played a significant part in producing her antagonistic behavior. Because Hans tried to leave her out of the meeting, his entourage of Western men followed suit.

It seems that authority in general flows more easily to men than to women, and in the case of culture at Transco, to Americans/Westerners than to Japanese. The problems go beyond those that occur simply as a result of the numerical dominance of American men at the top end of the corporation, although we have to start from there and work our way down through the organization. The kind of dominance that takes place at the top sets in motion a chain reaction effected through both gender and culture. People's schemas are weighted toward American culture and male gender whether they are trying to emulate the two or reacting against them as a defense mechanism. In addition, as will be shown below, there are subcultures at Transco that display these tendencies in the extreme, but no one seems to consider them a problem needing correction.

Gendered Versions of Marketing Presentations

The key members of Product Category C (hereafter PC-C) made their way into the room a few minutes ahead of the meeting with Walter. Most were from Marketing, with representatives also in attendance from Manufacturing, R&D, and Sales, who all were there primarily to confirm that the ideas put forth to Walter by those in Marketing were, in fact, logistically possible.

As soon as the meeting began, I realized I was witnessing yet another representation of subculture at Transco. I was made party to an idealized battle strategy, the proposed next step in a mock war. The metaphors were militaristic, the presentation including phrases like "the battlefield today" and "bleeding to death."

Unlike Product Category A (PC-A), which was more Japanese and female (this topic is discussed later in this chapter), PC-C was Western and male in orientation. Of the nine Marketing members present, seven were male; of these, three were *gaijin*, two of whom were in the top spots. The related staff from outside of Marketing was also mostly white males, including Finance and Manufacturing. The Western/male orientation of PC-C was an important point beyond the immediate membership; the category had a history of military maneuvers as metaphor that long outstripped the current makeup of personnel.

PC-C was fairing poorly in Japan. It had low market share and barely broke even monetarily. Although perceptions of marketing as a kind of battle are not uncommon to many companies, PC-C exhibited the tendency more than most, and when under siege, engaged in this behavior all the more. As might be expected, though Marketing in general was considered woman-friendly, the PC-C Marketing division was not. Female interviewees often clarified this point.

Although it is difficult to determine fully who should be doing the talking at Marketing presentations, in the case of PC-C (Marketing personnel only), the two Japanese women did not speak at all. Of the four Japanese men, one spoke not at all and two spoke rarely. The only regular participant was the more aggressive Japanese male mentioned in the earlier description of the middle managers meeting, and his participation was controlled by the two senior Western men in many of the same ways highlighted in the daylong product category meeting. He was interrupted frequently, his two superiors feeling the need to clarify his points. On one occasion, an apology for cutting him off was offered, but only once. However, this man clearly fit in well with the subculture of PC-C, whereas the other Japanese seemed more like outliers and the Japanese women seemed practically nonexistent.

The category was not so overcharged with aggression that its members could not pay proper respect to any authority or expertise; they did so very well to the senior white men. In an exchange between Walter and one of the *gaijin* in Marketing, for example, the *gaijin* was not afraid to disagree with Walter, but he always gave Walter the honor of finishing his sentence first, should the two of them start talking at the same time, before he went on to make his own point. Again, the scenario fit the profile of the daylong meeting: the Western men consciously gave one another their due but seemed to forget this behavior when their "opponents" were Japanese or female.

Coupled with this profile was the presumption that the Japanese always needed "help" in clarifying their points or making their arguments. It was a kind of culturally based paternalism patterned on the more common one for gender seen in corporate America. Transco bred both types of paternalism. Since both Japanese men and women were regarded as not yet ready for control of the company, a mandate to prepare them evolved. While perhaps a good thing in and of itself, it nonetheless created an imbalance of power at all levels of the organization. The Japanese became children of the adult American males. It was not recognized when Americans or males were the ones needing help from Japanese or females; it was presumed that only certain categories of employees were in need of training. The larger idea became entrenched in inappropriate ways and affected people's evaluations of one another. PC-C exhibited strong tendencies to assume that Americans and males were always correct in decision-making and other work-related behaviors, the exact same behavior seen in the daylong product category meeting.

Historically, I do not know whether PC-C evolved into a metaphoric war room to meet the needs of market success in a competitive industry, or whether it evolved as such simply to match the proclivities of a previous category leader. Regardless, PC-C had a reputation for being very "macho," which presumably affected who was assigned to work there. The question is, once a division takes such an aggressive masculine form, can it adapt to an alternative style if necessary to become competitive within a new set of circumstances? Or has it taken on a life of its own that precludes certain types of change?

The fact that PC-C had a long history of this behavior (outside of Japan, too) makes it more likely that it cannot change. For those who entered this Marketing category in Japan, they tended either to adapt or get out, especially women. There seemed to be no room for anybody else, even when the category was struggling to succeed. This kind of scenario created at least the potential for certain forms of male dominance, once established, to be set in stone, while other, smaller cultures within an organization would be regularly subject to change depending on the people contained within them.

To be fair, PC-C was not without its strong points. These were similar to those discussed earlier for American versus Japanese styles of communication—the aggressive style did lead to spirited exchange in which true brainstorming might occur. As Abe-san, who had once worked in PC-C, explained:

I think even now PC-C has more, how can I say, energy, reflecting the people there, due to the people there. [The people in my current category] are very mature in one sense; they are very cool in another sense. So they don't get too excited over small things. They take most things into their mind for consideration without too much complaining, or too much speaking up with a different point of view. PC-C, again reflecting the persons there, they tend to say whatever they feel, even if it is somewhat a stupid point. But I tend to feel less energy in [my current category], and that makes me worried. Because sometimes,

even if [something] is stupid, the energy drives the motivation, the energy drives the progress, the working progress.

Abe-san went on to say that he was looking to bring PC-C–type
people into his category to gain some of the energy he saw there
but had thus far not been successful because the tenor of his current place was markedly different. Abe-san noted that his personal
(cooler) style was quite similar to that of his boss, a Western male.
This similarity, I think, lends credence to the power of senior managers to set the (sub)culture of their respective divisions; once
characterized in a particular way, change is slow in coming. The
problem for women in general and Japanese at Transco is that similar types of subcultures are in operation that favor the traits associated with males and Western culture. In the same way that people's
personalities may not be able to transcend the culture that dominates their division (and in the case of PC-C, women would look
very strange acting like soldiers in a battle even if their personalities
matched this norm), women and Japanese cannot transcend the
dominant culture that continues to favor American(ized) males in
the overall.

By way of comparison to PC-C, when the PC-A team met with
Walter to pitch its vision, the mood was decidedly different. For one
thing, though there was a smaller portion of PC-A in attendance for
the meeting with Walter, PC-A in the overall had greater numbers of
women, including the all-woman Marketing team, and fewer *gaijin*,
than PC-C. The PC-A meetings that I attended always were similar
to those that Abe-san described for his category, mature in a certain
way and cool in another. An important exception is Ono-san, who,
as one leader of PC-A, was inclined to displays of bad temper, but
unlike PC-C where Japanese seemed to try to adopt the style of the
senior Western males, people in PC-A knew it was a good idea not to
copy at least this aspect of Ono-san's style. The coolly mature sentiment seemed to prevail as a Japanese style nonetheless.

The lead figures from Marketing in this presentation to Walter
were Ono-san and Igawa-san. All others present were male, one
Korean new to Marketing in Japan, and people from related divisions: a Japanese from Sales, and a Korean and an American from

Finance. Everyone seemed to participate more fully at this meeting. It had a calmer tone, more like a discussion than a presentation designed to win over Walter. It was more formal than the presentation made by PC-C but not without considerable joking, especially between Igawa-san and Walter.

Igawa-san seemed very comfortable at the meeting. She asserted herself in the quiet way that marks her nature, and Walter was quite complimentary toward her performance. He also offered to "protect" her from Hans (mentioned earlier in this chapter as being in an antagonistic relationship with Walter) if he continued to pressure one of Igawa-san's teams solely on the basis of a price reduction.

The most noticeable aspect of the meeting was that Ono-san acted part of the time just like the problematic American men (and the American/Western women who join them on occasion) I have described throughout this chapter. She cut off both her peers and her subordinates, corrected them without necessarily knowing where they were going, told them what to do in an abrupt manner ("just answer this question"; "just give him this info"), but she also monitored their participation, translated for them if they were having difficulty comprehending the discussion, and explained to them what the point was if they did not understand.

In short, she exhibited many of the worse traits of the more paternalistic American males but also some of the best traits of the Japanese in general and the more conscientious Americans. So the question again is, why was she singled out among the many for these negative behavioral traits? The answers are (1) because she was female and her division was struggling, and (2) because she was female, period.

If she was still riding the high wave of marketing success that characterized her previous years, these bad traits would have been, indeed were, overlooked. But once her division started to struggle, people—her superiors in particular—started to look for explanations, and her "other-ness" came to the fore. She was not a good example of a "female" leader; she is not the least bit maternal. To make matters worse, she acted paternal much of the time.

Whether in charge of a division that is struggling or succeeding, women are not allowed the same terrain of behavior as men.

Their range is much smaller; thus they will be judged in the negative for straying much sooner. The paternalistic male is acceptable, but men can also behave without regard for other people in the immediate context of meetings as well as in the longer-term context of getting away with a "less than optimal" personality. Men who display too much aggression or disregard for others may eventually be drummed out of the organization, but only if they are not successful in other ways. Even in this, they have much wider room for their behavior, will last much longer without accruing sanctions, and will be judged to be bad employees rather than bad men.

Thus, socialization on the basis of gender and culture continues in the transnational organization. It must be pointed out that women are guilty of these charges, too. When senior management women train other women, they have to choose between conforming to the accepted definitions of gender and culture appropriateness or challenging them. Many times women do not see conformation as a problem, and if they do, it is safer to acquiesce and remain in alignment with their male peers. Authority is made manifest by one's position in the organization, but the manifestation does not escape close association with the culture and gender of the person occupying that position.

6 Embracing Chaos: Toward a More Genuine Valuation of Difference

The corporation that includes Transco as a subsidiary increasingly sees itself as global, not just in Japan but everywhere, because it equates giving a directive ("Let's go global," to use Nobu-san's wording) with achieving a result. While such an equation may work for any number of directives, it does not and cannot work for a directive to go global. In the first place, senior managers cannot really describe what this means at the level of human resources even if they can describe it at the level of production and distribution. Senior managers themselves are not global employees in their perceptions and understanding of a global person—they have been assigned to different points around the globe but were not necessarily ever challenged to become a global person. Relatedly, as numerous employees pointed out to me, "Let's go global" comes down from the top and as it filters down, each manager gives it her or his personal stamp based on her or his understanding of what it means—implying that each stamp also contains her or his lack of understanding as to the meaning of *globalization*.

This increase in nebulous meaning (*globalization*) augments the tendency to rely on stereotypes when evaluating personnel to achieve some kind of clarity upon which managers feel they can act. What is needed is the reverse: to clarify what the *globalization* of human resources means and eliminate stereotypes as a tool for assessment of employee effectiveness. Lack of clarity in terms such as *globalization* also enables senior management to avoid defining itself. This omission perpetuates a tendency on the part of senior management to assume little variation of any kind within itself when, in fact, outside of nationality and gender, the variation is widespread. If senior management recognized its own variations as to style, personality, and personal principles of management, it could judge better the qualities desired in all employees without resorting to facile formulas that force individuals into opposing pairs of boxes.[1]

Just before the completion of this final chapter, I investigated the whereabouts of all six of my primary subjects,[2] to learn whether their subsequent career paths continued to conform with one basic argument of this book, namely that culture and gender are (mis)applied in similar patterns that serve as convenient justifications for the positive or negative evaluation of employees *as needed*. Positive (mis)applications are problematic primarily because they perpetuate patterns of stereotypic thought and open the door to negative (mis)applications, making it easier for someone to be pushed through that door. Once someone falls under the weight of negative (mis)applications of culture or gender, it is very difficult, if not impossible, to escape; a bubble surrounds the employee and dominates everyone's perceptions no matter how the employee tries to present her or his self. All levels of employees are capable of exhibiting these patterns, but senior executives have the power to make or break careers on the basis of them.

As a reminder, originally five of the six were considered to be good candidates for further promotion, while Ono-san, the highest-ranking Japanese woman whose further prospects did not look good before my fieldwork began, was on her way out of the organization once she reached General Management. Of the six, four remain at Transco.

Igawa-san did, in fact, move off the line leading to General Management into an expert position in Advertising, in keeping with her intentions at the time of my fieldwork to steer herself away from the excessive pressures of Marketing and have better opportunities for work/family balance. Her expertise in Marketing makes her a valuable addition to her new division and she is well positioned to advance further in this arena. She remains single, but for her, work/family balance also included not having to work on the weekend.

The two women who were not particularly attached to Transco as a lifetime endeavor have done quite well. Watanabe-san, who thought she might someday switch to social work, moved up to Marketing Director of a different division and within the last two years advanced further to General Management. She also married and became a mother. Okura-san, who claims to put family first, has also continued to advance within Research and Development. She went on assignment to the United States for a couple of years, returned to Japan in an advanced position, and will soon move to Asia-wide responsibilities as a further promotion. And Nobu-san, our casual dresser, changed divisions within Research and Development and received a promotion to Director. He maintains his strong outside interests, particularly in music.

Ono-san did, in fact, "retire" from Transco though she did not want to leave the company. She had a number of starts at other high-ranking jobs before settling on the entrepreneurial freedom of her own consulting business, with a special focus on global marketing. Her business has turned out to be successful, and she serves mainly a Japanese clientele. She also publishes and gives lectures related to her current and previous work; one lecture that I attended in Japan in late 2006 was held in a rather large room that filled to capacity with Japanese men outnumbering Japanese women by a fair margin. Her direct style of speech and manner was evident in her Japanese-language presentation; I worried that some in the audience might be put off by her style, but the lengthy question-and-answer session after the talk made clear that her style was not alienating. Ono-san seems also to have rediscovered much of her "Japanese-ness" through a number of traditional cultural pursuits; in many ways she has become the dual persona that worked well for many women at Transco.

Abe-san, who was described initially by his boss as "typically Japanese," also did not want to leave Transco but is now gone. Walter and Abe-san's immediate (EM) supervisor viewed him as a promising candidate for further promotion, despite their assessment that his performance flaws were rooted in his national culture. However, when it came time to move "up" in rank "or out" of the company altogether, he was reportedly steered toward the latter against his will. He first worked for one American company in Japan and then landed another job at one of the largest American multinationals in the world. His case warrants the further commentary given in this section.

I am not in a position, nor is it my intention, to state that the dismissals of Abe-san and Ono-san were mistakes on the part of senior management, nor can I determine that the promotions or lateral transfers of the other four were correct. Profit and loss and other kinds of calculations may well prove that each candidate deserved what he or she received. What I am interested in is the process of thought involved, especially in the case first of Ono-san and now of Abe-san. In both cases their respective personalities as "aggressive" and "typically Japanese" were known all along, yet both moved steadily up in rank, Ono-san for twenty years and Abe-san for ten years.

In the case of Ono-san, it is fair to assume that her aggressive personality was positively evaluated in her early years at Transco at least insofar as she was responsible for a number of huge marketing successes at a time when Transco was really struggling to succeed in Japan. However, at the level of senior management, it became her greatest drawback. Because I have spent a lot of time on Ono-san, knowing that she was on her way out of the organization, I will add only the following installment from my field notes.

At a meeting I attended early in the fieldwork with Ono-san, Igawa-san, and Jack, the corporate-wide head of Research and Development who was visiting from the United States, he was very apologetic and told her that she should have stood her ground against a man who had left her uninformed about some key product information during a meeting the day before. He also reported to her that he told the man never to do it again. Ono-san responded with a joke that the "normal" Ono-san would have blown up, but that the "new" Ono-san, fresh from a performance evaluation in which she was told to act more like a woman, tries to keep cool no matter what. He continued to insist that she should get in there "and push" and refuse to take that kind of treatment, to which Ono-san replied, "Being a woman, I cannot do that." He offered to help her as needed.

This man did not work with Ono-san on a regular basis and thus was not in a position to use the lens through which Walter and others were viewing her, even if he was aware of that lens through conversations with them; he appraised the situation at face value and encouraged her to fight back, not knowing that heeding the advice he was giving her would only lead to further estrangement from the senior management with whom she did work. So how, exactly, was Ono-san suppose to behave on the job? Which message was the correct one?

To review the case of Abe-san, we can analyze the characterizations that supposedly made him "typically Japanese." He was said to be quiet, reserved, and careful, possessing a Japanese sense of time (which his boss translated as meaning he did not push urgency and gave his subordinates too much time to do their work), and was too hands off with his subordinates (meaning that he did not differentiate between those that needed more help and those that did not). His performance was considered "great" but taking too long to achieve the results. Is there any benefit to considering all of this "typically Japanese" behavior?

In my field notes, I recorded the following observations in a meeting between Abe-san and me and one between Abe-san and one of his subordinates. For our meeting, I noted that he was more talkative and friendly than his boss said he would be. I also recorded that he took a different approach from Ono-san in setting me up to observe him. Whereas Ono-san simply handed me her schedule and let me determine which things I would attend, Abe-san suggested that he pick the meetings. I went along, believing that I could alter his suggestions if I felt I needed to do so, but "his picks were varied and numerous, carefully selected to try to match my needs, and gave me a degree of choice." With Abe-san, I ended up with the same extensive access that I had with Ono-san (and all the others). He never refused any request that I made; it is just that he tried to be conscientious about my research agenda.

In one of the meetings with a subordinate who was having difficulties completing his work, Abe-san repeatedly said things to his subordinate such as "I don't think we have to keep discussing that between the two of us. If you feel uncomfortable, let's meet with the creative people today or tomorrow," "You don't have to always follow my time pressure—I leave it to you to manage your time productively," "Sorry to say this, but you should have . . . ," "You don't have to do a thorough analysis; it must be simple," "I think I explained (this) clearly to you before," and "Very honestly, I encourage you to use the (such and such) data, especially if the data manipulation you are doing requires so much time."

I noted that based on my observations the subordinate seemed determined not to receive the messages Abe-san was sending, and I wondered if he was one of the people Abe-san's boss thought needed more rather than less help. But it appeared that Abe-san *was* providing him with the help he needed, coaching him on more effective use of his time and criticizing him for focusing on the wrong things, albeit in a less than forceful manner. I observed Abe-san giving extended guidance to other subordinates on occasion, some of whom may not have needed it, and I watched him examine subordinates' written materials very carefully and ask many questions, but I never equated this with his being "typically Japanese" even though I was prompted to do so. I am also quite sure that Ono-san's approach with the slow subordinate would have been to phrase things much more severely ("You are wasting time doing this," "This is useless," and perhaps even "You are not stupid, so why are you doing such a stupid thing?"), but her approach was deemed wrong, too. Is Transco therefore looking for something in between the two approaches, and would it not be more beneficial to focus on the specifics of the desired approach rather than the culture or gender of the person being evaluated? Is any employee ever characterized as "typically American" or told to act "more like a man?" And even if these types of comments were to be made, exactly what would either one mean as a positive or a negative?

In the remainder of this final chapter I would like to address these kinds of questions along with several of those with which I began this study (see Chapter 1). In doing so, I will draw together some of the major findings of this research and suggest several possible solutions and directions.

Perceptions

At Transco, Japanese men and women in management, Japanese secretaries, and the expatriated (American) management perceive themselves and one another across a number of gender and cultural boundaries. These perceptions, in tandem with those growing out of the nature of one's job position in the organization, determine each person's perceptions of authority.

To start from the top of the organization, EMs arrive in Japan feeling that they need to assert themselves as leaders. Establishing their authority means setting a new agenda that is largely imparted to subordinates with little room for input. They are too busy, and the organization does not reward them for the time it would require to learn Japanese and understand Japan as a cultural entity in its own right. They rely on secretaries to help them function in their daily lives both in and out of the office and in many cases avoid the "real" Japan as much as possible, establishing instead the stereotypic life of an expatriated citizen. They represent themselves at work as knowledgeable about the business side of things, and they are, but they perhaps downplay the importance of knowledge about Japan in the process.

In addition, EMs are affected by the belief on the part of senior management that neither Japanese men nor Japanese women at Transco are ready for unassisted control of the company. Thus EMs assume that they themselves are the best the company has to offer, reinforcing the likelihood of self-replication at the higher levels. Legitimization of the belief is rooted in formulations of cultural binaries in which Americans are what Japanese are not, as reflected, for example, in Walter's chart on the essential differences between the two cultures (presented in Chapter 4).

With the arrival of a new EM, the Japanese employees focus their attention on his limited understanding of Japan. They see him as someone who will push on them an uninformed agenda without utilizing the expertise that they could lend. They see him as someone who will not bother to learn about Japan—their culture—beyond a superficial level. And they criticize the company for fostering this type of EM.

Japanese men in management further resent the constant arrival of EMs because they feel they have to prove themselves over and over. They are concerned with the lack of control they feel within the context of so much change. They argue for continuity in ideas and in personnel. *Continuity* is a concept that, in the traditional Japanese corporation, would reward them simply for being men with tenure in the corporation. Their preference for continuity and their approval of the "Japanese way of doing" in this regard exists despite the fact that many of them come to Transco in search of rewards based on merit rather than seniority.

Globalization as a corporate directive is particularly threatening to Japanese men at Transco because it creates a similar type of uncertainty that they frame in a cross-cultural context. They see the Americans in corporate headquarters (based in the United States) as people who also jump on ideas to make a personal mark without enough regard for the effects at the lower levels, especially in subsidiaries outside the United States. It is, in their view, up to the Japanese to straighten out the problems at Transco caused by what they see as sweeping changes in directions and repetitions of error.

Japanese women in management are more consistent in their desire for an alternative workplace in Japan and thus have more positive evaluations of both American culture and American management, even though they recognize many of the same downsides. At Transco, they are more likely to feel that they will be rewarded for doing a good job without regard to gender. They resolve some of their sense of difference from the Japanese norm for women by working in a foreign corporation. Where they felt uncomfortable as a child and even in college, now they feel much more positive about themselves as individual Japanese. They are quick to credit particular EMs, as well as foreign experience, with their personal development. This better fit with the corporation predisposes them to take a more positive view of Americans and American culture. As a result, they are less threatened by constant change in the work environment.

For these women, however, gender as a factor in the assessment, both internal and external, of their performance can increasingly come into play as they move up the corporate ladder. As they rise in the organization, the pressure increases, and they work with greater numbers of expatriated management. Failure of any kind creates the possibility that their gender will come into question as a causal factor, as was the case with Ono-san on a number of occasions with more than one EM. On a personal level, though they consistently rank themselves as more satisfied than their Japanese male peers with the company and their jobs/careers, they also consistently rank themselves well below their male peers when it comes to satisfaction with the performance and career guidance they are receiving and with work/family balance.

Bilingual secretaries return us once again to the top of the organization. Though they share many of the negative Japanese male attitudes toward the cultural proclivities of the EMs, they nonetheless perceive the organization as a whole from the perspective of their bosses and try to negotiate smooth relations between respective members of the two cultures. They are comfortable in both the American and Japanese cultural contexts, often adopting a teaching role vis-à-vis their expatriated bosses, and by virtue of being secretaries they do not face many of the same struggles that Japanese women in management encounter as they attempt to move up the line.

Theories of occupational sex segregation offer some explanation for the difficulties managerial women in general have with moving up the corporate ladder, and in the case of the transnational corporation, segregation based on nationality may also occur. Bielby and Baron posit that "sex segregation is built into the hierarchy of organizational positions and is sustained by sex stereotypes and workplace social relations" (1986, p. 760). The American nationality and male gender of the expatriated management situated at the top of Transco's hierarchy produced the dominant stereotypes that occurred at that level, but these stereotypes, in turn, filtered down through the organization and affected the perceptions of all employees.

Negotiations

Certain problems are perhaps inherent to Transco's hybrid habitus, but the solutions exist within that same hybridity. There is a constant interplay of cultural forces at Transco. The culture of the parent organization dominates the subsidiary, but conformation and resistance occur simultaneously. The Japanese adapt to the cultural dictates "sent down" by the senior American management but then also engage in aborting the cultural dictates from the bottom up, creating negative sanctions, such as the *Trans-toid* label, for those who appear to adapt too much.

Japanese women must adapt to both gender and cultural dictates. They respond better than the Japanese men to the cultural environment of Transco in part because they are seeking a better gender environment than they feel would exist at a native Japanese corporation. Thus they perhaps want to adapt more than the men do, and the American management thought that they did adapt better. However, in each employee creation of Transco's culture, some people get left out while others find a place. Thus, as can be seen in the women's development program, some women who used to belong were now on the outskirts while others moved to the center. The cultural fit of different sets of people is oddly situational; yet it is the organization that is creating the various situations to which the Japanese must adapt, all the while decrying Japanese culture for its situational tendencies.

Because senior American management believes in absolutes, they do not see the culturally relative situations they create. What they see are some Japanese employees who adapt "well" to Transco and some who do not. This scenario leads to the potential for overvaluing Japanese employees who most act like Americans and devaluing those who do not. The Japanese know this valuation on some level and want to appear to be succeeding along Transco's cultural lines, and women are even likely to feel that this type of success is good for them even if they do not quite understand it. But the Japanese also counter Transco's culture by creating an opposing system of evaluation that privileges their own culture. Many people feel caught in the middle of these opposing environments and struggle with how to behave at work.

Japanese women tend to feel more comfortable than their male counterparts operating in both worlds, though they adopt a variety of strategies for doing so, including the creation of dual personas, one for work and one for home. Many people, especially women, appear to "blossom" at the company, but as a result, they may face being labeled as *Trans-toids* by other, more typically Japanese coworkers. Ironically, just as women finally are resolving one sense of difference, their coworkers establish for them yet another. Where once they felt they were not typical Japanese females, now they are told they are not good Japanese. Cultural sanctions replace gender sanctions, but there remain gender ramifications to the *Trans-toid* label insofar as more men use it to sanction women who appear to be doing well at the company.

In contrast to some of the managerial women, bilingual secretaries did not describe feelings of difference from mainstream Japanese women. They came to Transco more in search of a place to utilize their language skills; the vast majority are happy being bilingual secretaries and do not try to change careers. Most of them find the dual culture easy to negotiate.

Bilingual secretaries have fewer problems in part because their role is to help the management rather than to become like the management. Particularly as women they are fulfilling more clearly understood gender roles—there is little confusion as to how a secretary is supposed to behave. Secretaries do have to negotiate the cultural conflict at Transco but not in a way that threatens their sense of security about their jobs. Since they plan to remain secretaries, their work will be more or less the same and their promotions will be based more on whom they are working for and less on the work itself. Thus their cultural concerns have more to do with creating a fit between their Americanized work lives and their Japanese home lives. To create this fit, secretaries were more likely to develop dual personas than the managerial women.

Another important issue that divides Japanese secretaries from their managerial counterparts is the nature of their authority. They do glean authority from their bosses, but in their day-to-day work environment, they also have one of the most important authority traits, fluency in English. Not only do their expatriated bosses become dependent on them for interaction with things Japanese outside of Transco, they can often communicate better than the managerial Japanese can with the expatriated management. They are able to feel successful because their English language ability is one of their most important status and authority markers. Managerial Japanese must develop this same capability, but they do not necessarily enter the organization fluent in English as the bilingual secretaries do. Language becomes part of the contest over authority among the management.[3]

Thus the messages about culture and gender are mixed, and the Japanese are left to negotiate the constantly changing landscape. Gender and culture biases in operation at Transco may not be addressed as fully as they need to be because people do not see that patterns of authority and recognition of merit are stacked differentially within the system. If you are white and male at Transco, you benefit from a number of intangibles.

Further, the proclivities of senior males are still not addressed at all. American men in particular have significant advantages over others because their style of interaction already fits in well with the culture of Transco. They are also more likely to rely on other American or Western men to bolster their sense of leadership and belonging. In a room, faced with the presence of groups of women and Japanese nationals, Western men look to other Western men upon whom they can depend for similarity of ideas and approach. They presume that commonality exists among similar types and that differences exist between them and other categories. If they are insecure, either from within based on personality or from without based on weaknesses in their division, they tend to exaggerate differences even more rather than look for a new approach.

The dominant presence of American men at the top of the organization legitimates a paternalistic attitude on both culture and gender vectors throughout the organization, and this same paternalism is said to exist for gender at world headquarters in the United States. There is a reflexive tendency always to "help" the Japanese employee. One's status as an American or Western male lends an air of legitimacy; this category is presumed to be the one most likely to know how to do things the Transco way. Even when the Japanese have something specific to offer, it may be overlooked, and the system permits, perhaps even encourages, these types of omission.

Japanese women have to negotiate gender in addition to culture. Subject to all of the same cultural patterns at Transco by which the Japanese are thought to need help, women are further constrained to stay within the acceptable bounds of their gender. Being more quiet and low key keeps them from being sanctioned like Ono-san, but then they are likely to be ignored even when lending a certain type of recognized expertise. (American) men can display more aggressive forms of authority with little likelihood of sanctions. Their gender is rarely, if ever, considered as an explanation for their behavior or their poor on-the-job performance. Conditioned to take advantage of a system already stacked in their favor, they fail to see the gender and culture privileges in ready operation at Transco.

Chaos and Its Logic

In many ways, to dialogue successfully across difference[4] in the transnational corporation is to embrace certain elements of chaos but not for the sake of chaos itself. One has to see the inherent logic of that chaos, and make changes from that point of view. Understanding the chaos can be particularly beneficial to organizations such as Transco. Not only is the parent corporation situated geographically all around the globe, there are many complex variations of personnel that lead to any number of culture and gender conundrums that hinder employees' full assumption of the authority attendant to their managerial positions in the organization.

Chaos theory originated in mathematics and physics but has also been applied to the study of organizations.[5] Application to culture and gender draws upon many of the same principles; most important for our purposes is the idea that self-organization will occur out of disequilibrium. Senior managers set certain types of disequilibrium in motion from the top down when they differentially apply personal "rules" for dealing with people outside their own gender and culture. Lower-level employees reorganize what comes down in whatever ways they need to do to reassert their sense of worth. This type of chaos is not welcomed.

The chaos that should be encouraged is one in which binaries are actively rooted out of the organization, leaving people to reorganize themselves in ways that avoid easy reliance on stereotypical conceptualizations of Americans versus Japanese and men versus women. If we return to the idea presented in the introduction that differences among those in any one group are far greater than the differences between groups, management of people needs to be focused on accepting and encouraging the "differences among" and diminishing reliance on assumed "differences between." This task is not as hard as it might seem, but it has to start at the top of the organization. As mentioned previously, Transco's senior managers were more effective transnational thinkers when it came to products and less effective transnational thinkers when it came to people. Because senior managers were not transnational themselves when it came to human resources, they could not model this behavior and thinking for their subordinates.

The binomial patterns of thought concerning culture and gender that are evident in Transco's approaches to human resources prevent the development of transnational thinking because it, by definition, cannot be based on binaries. Simple geographic dispersion of subsidiaries can tolerate cultural binomials. Although I would argue that gendered binaries are problematic wherever they exist because they subvert both men's and women's achievement of performance excellence, for culture it depends on what type of organization the corporation wants to be.

As the Japanese subsidiary of an American corporation engaged in a strategic series of moves toward *globalization*, Transco faces its own particular set of issues. While following the dictates set by the parent organization in the United States, it must attend to the reality of employing mostly Japanese nationals and operating within the Japanese national context. A key issue lies in how Transco defines this reality.

The parent organization views itself as being very favorable to employee diversity of all types, but its organizational culture originates within the context of American national culture, where diversity of national culture is less of an issue than diversity of gender, race, ethnicity, and sexual orientation. Unlike Transco, the parent organization is not facing daily struggles rooted in the conflict between national cultures, although it will face this issue in the future if globalization proceeds in full measure.

Most of the thinking about the directions that Transco needs to take comes from senior American management sent to Japan for a few years. They have moved up in the parent organization because they exhibited many of the ideal traits valued by the senior officers in the United States and (even if they did not exhibit the ideal traits) because their performance was linked to profitability. The expatriated managers are presumed to understand the priorities of the parent organization, including profitability, and are themselves products of its organizational culture. Thus the culture of the parent organization dominates the subsidiary by virtue of the expatriated management.

Though Transco is expected to be reflective of the parent organization, adaptation nevertheless occurs both intentionally and unintentionally. Transco is perceived differently by the Japanese employees than it is by the expatriated management; among the Japanese, it is perceived differently by women than by men; and among women, it is not the same for those in management as it is for those who serve as bilingual secretaries. Each group comes to Transco with its own set of requirements and goals, and Transco's organizational culture constitutes itself through the interactions among them all.

Conflict and confusion are inherent to the formation of Transco's organizational culture, and they are intensified by the fact that within groups individual variation in beliefs and attitudes also occurs. Yet there are group characteristics that individual members shared.

Japanese women in management generally feel that Transco is a good place for women compared to what might be available in a native Japanese corporation. They are also more likely to describe feelings of difference from the Japanese norm for women and are seeking to work for an organization that rewards them for being different by providing them with better career opportunities. The numbers of Japanese women seeking careers will continue to increase; in the almost daily statistics that arise from Japan, female college graduates, just the demographic that Transco targets, are eschewing marriage more than ever before.[6] Because they hold negative views of Japanese corporations' treatment of managerial women, Japanese women who work at Transco tend to see the company in a positive light, even when they experience problems or are dissatisfied with aspects of work such as the career guidance they receive during personnel reviews.

Japanese men in management are attracted to Transco's professed system of merit as the basis for promotions, unlike Japanese women who simply are looking for fair treatment relative to men. As the campaign of globalization unfolds, however, Japanese men evince a greater concern for the negative ramifications of globalization, and they consider the ways in which native Japanese corporations might be outperforming Transco, such as providing a feeling of continuity in the organization. Because they, unlike Japanese women, can see themselves potentially as faring better in a native Japanese corporation, they are less positive about Transco and more prone to complain about the cultural imbalances they see in the organization.

Bilingual secretaries, all of whom are Japanese women, come to Transco to be secretaries. Rather than a career in management, they are looking for a place in which their English language skills can be used, and they arrive at the organization linguistically ready to negotiate the mixed culture. Though they seem among the most comfortable at Transco in many ways, bilingual secretaries hold attitudes in common with Japanese employees regarding the nature of the expatriated management, and they sympathize with Japanese men in management who view the regular rotation of expatriated managers as culturally problematic to the organization. Yet the "helplessness" of the expatriated management vis-à-vis "things Japanese" confers on bilingual secretaries a kind of power unavailable to other Japanese at Transco, and some secretaries take it upon themselves to try to educate their bosses about "how things work" both in Japan and in Transco itself.

The expatriated managers are likely to arrive in Japan with an eye to making their personal mark before moving on to their next assignment. They have "new" ideas for implementation and are not as willing to learn how things previously had been done (both right and wrong) as their Japanese subordinates hope they would be. Although they are interested in learning about Japan, and many of them study Japanese, these efforts are minimal in comparison to the time spent on their "real" jobs, and the parent organization in any case does not reward them for such achievements. The EMs are aware that in a few years they will likely be sent to another country.

The senior American (male) management characterizes the Japanese employees as "not yet ready" to take the reins of the corporation, sometimes describing a parental relationship for themselves vis-à-vis the Japanese employees, whom they view as children en route to becoming proper corporate adults who could well manage the Japan operations. Such perceptions then augment the tendency to prefer Americans for top leadership positions in Japan, and these Americans generally are white and male.

The expatriated managers are in large agreement over the areas of cultural "improvement" necessary before the Japanese can assume full control of the subsidiary. To understand and make decisions about the changes needed at Transco, they tend to analyze the organization in terms of cultural binaries that relegate certain American characteristics to a superior status in comparison to their Japanese opposites. Having absolute values is better than having situational ones, and being frank is better than being reserved.

Group Formation and Individual Identity

The existence of at least some group characteristics provides the means for an internal coherence to the chaotic elements that mark Transco. Although the culture of the parent organization does dominate at Transco, the kinds of cultural adaptations that occur, as well as the ways in which the dominant culture is subverted by pockets of opposing subcultures, depends on group formation.

A single person designating another person a *Trans-toid* would have little effect on the organization as a whole, but a number of people engaging in such behavior has an effect that changes the organizational culture. People are more likely to behave differently because of the threat of being labeled a *Trans-toid,* even if only to decide to ignore the appellation.

Each group, therefore, contributes to the formation of the particular organizational culture of Transco, to the types of opposition that occur, and to the chaos that ensues. The expatriated management presents Transco as a place in which all would be evaluated fairly on the basis of merit, but merit itself is laden with characteristics drawn from American ideas about culture and gender. Being "too Japanese" is not a source of merit, but acting "like an American" is. The Japanese culture displayed by many employees is considered to contain problematic elements that need to be fixed.

The Japanese respond by situating many characteristics of American culture in a negative light when compared to opposing Japanese traits. Americans are said to be immoderate, inconsiderate, and unable to listen. The expatriated management is regarded as lacking understanding of the "real Japan," and they are criticized for not learning Japanese and for requiring the use of English even when it might impede Japanese understanding of important issues related to daily life at Transco.

The Japanese also create a boundary line for appropriate behavior as a Japanese. Crossing too far over to the American side of the line leaves one subject to cultural sanction by being labeled a *Trans-toid.* Being adept at negotiating American culture is negatively linked to a willingness to forego one's status as a "good" Japanese national.

The *Trans-toid* label further becomes one means by which Japanese men separate themselves from and try to control Japanese women. More women than men are labeled *Trans-toids,* and more men than women apply the label to others. This is reflective of the fact that Japanese women appear better able than Japanese men to adapt to the corporate culture.

Senior American management also thinks that Japanese women are better at the necessary cultural adaptation, but women who are "too aggressive" face problems as they reach the higher levels of the organization, with some being advised to display more appropriate qualities of "female leadership." Thus women more successfully negotiate the culture of Transco only to face gender requirements for successful on-the-job performance at the higher levels of the organization.

To many of the women who desire long-term managerial careers at Transco, Japanese culture appears too confining. They assume they would do better in an American corporation in the type of work they would perform and in their chances for upward mobility. Compared to the situation for women who currently work in native Japanese corporations, these opportunities appear largely to be true.

Women hold many of the same jobs as the men and move up to and through middle management in this foreign corporation, but there are inequalities as well. The numbers of women are not well represented in several divisions, and the percentage of women managers in divisions where their numbers are well represented is low compared to their male counterparts. Thus Japanese women seem to face gender constraints even in this Americanized work context. They are not necessarily rewarded as well as the men for negotiating the cultural divide, even though they tend to perform better in this regard, because their female gender serves as a separate constraint that can become operant with little warning. Whereas Japanese men and women both contend with cultural distinctions, Japanese women also contend with gender distinctions.

Japanese men can see themselves in greater numbers than women throughout the corporation, with the express exception of secretaries (and beauty consultants who work in the field). Cultural conflict constitutes the greatest threat to their sense of place within the organization, but there are few places that Japanese men do not appear to belong. The only obstacle seems to be senior management, and because senior managers comprise primarily American expatriates, virtually of one ilk in cultural representation, corporate culture as it reflects the tension between American and Japanese culture becomes the primary concern of Japanese men.

Japanese women not only see that they are not in senior management but also that they are differentially placed within departments and divisions. Certain departments have quite a few women; others barely have any. Within departmental divisions, the proportion of women also varies considerably. There are divisions within which men not only dominate numerically but also subscribe to a "macho" ethic for behavior. Few women either enter or remain in these male domains.

As is true for many companies, Marketing is a division from which Transco routinely draws the largest number of corporate leadership prospects. Moving up in Marketing leads to senior positions in General Management. Marketing demands a wide variety of skills, both qualitative and quantitative, that are necessary to management of the corporation as a whole. It is also a division in which one can more readily make a name for oneself, as there is a clear link between a successful marketing campaign and an increase in corporate profits. Conversely, there is a negative link when profit share declines.

Marketing is also one of the more stressful divisions. People often describe the work as "warlike" in nature, composed of campaigns to battle against other companies for a greater share of consumer spending. Indeed, a number of the Marketing presentations to senior management that I witnessed, in particular those from brand groups comprising mostly men (especially Western men), were replete with the metaphors of war. By comparison, presentations by brand groups dominated by women were quite dissimilar, despite the fact that women, too, spoke to me of marketing as a kind of war.

The conundrum for women in Marketing is part and parcel of this war-room mentality. The company ultimately penalizes women for personalities that are, essentially, too warlike, despite the fact that these types of women are drawn to Marketing in the first place and successful in their jobs in part because of their strong personalities. Both Ono-san and the other woman mentioned as having problems after she returned from the United States were from Marketing and interested in long-term careers that led to senior management of Transco. Less aggressive women were preferred by senior management, but these same women were less interested in advancing beyond middle management.

Gender and Authority within the Cultural Matrix of Organization and Nation

For corporations that operate around the globe and rely primarily on local citizens to fill their employee ranks in each country, cross-cultural interaction further complicates the human-to-human relationships at work by providing yet another bifurcated lens through which employees look at themselves and one another. Unlike gender relations, however, where numerous theorists argue that the cultural self is represented by the male while the female represents the cultural other, in cross-cultural relations there remains a constant battle for the terrain of self, each side perceiving the other as other. Because the bifurcation of views as a method of considering one's place in the world is similar to both culture and gender, it is possible that a parallel study of both within the context of an organization may lead to a broader understanding of the constraints that such bifurcation causes.

Gender issues in the workplace are also manifested in the behavior of employees. The gender division at a particular workplace is itself a structure that constrains the positioning of new men and women who enter the company. But it is important to draw a distinction between gender-based structures and gender-based behaviors. A belief in the latter often has served as an excuse for the existence of the former, but the behavior is more likely to be the result of gender discrimination rather than innate behavioral differences between men and women.

Kanter's (1977) site-based study of the role of men and women in an American corporation looks at the ramifications of corporate culture in terms of gendered workplace aspirations and structured occupational behaviors. It is a study that still holds sway today. One key argument is that numerical imbalance of the sexes at various levels of occupations within the corporation leads to predictable behaviors in *human beings*, regardless of gender, thus disputing notions of "female" versus "male" styles and replacing them with the styles of "tokens" versus "dominants" and the like. The workplace behavior of men and women is more likely to be explained by their relative numbers within occupations than by gendered proclivities to act in certain ways: "Men and women of the corporation, then, relate to each other and to their work through jobs that are often sex-segregated and laden with idealized images of the capacities of the people in them. These views define the principal players" (p. 28).

In Kanter's research, men (as dominants) assigned four roles— mother, pet, seductress, iron maiden—to women (as tokens). To create a framework for dealing with women as an unknown element in managerial interaction, men relied on stereotypes drawn from the larger culture. The women were, in essence, forced to conform to the roles assigned to them. This role playing enabled dominants "to make use of already-learned expectations and modes of action, like the traditional ways men expect to treat women," but also "can serve to keep tokens in a bounded place and out of the mainstream of interaction" (p. 230).

More recent evidence suggests that women may be responding differently to their status as tokens, expanding the overall number of roles and even exerting some element of personal choice as to which roles they play. However, the roles remain limited and limiting, particularly in regard to the necessity for some type of decision about sexuality at work, whether to emphasize or hide one's sexual differences from men.[7]

At Transco I did not see evidence of managerial women's need to make decisions about sexuality at work, with the important (and rather ironic) exception of the development program for women in management, but tokenism certainly plays out across both culture and gender lines. The American management places Japanese managers of both genders into stereotypes based on their relative distance from Americanized behavior; the closer the employee is to the American end of the behavioral spectrum, the more likely he or she is to receive a positive work evaluation from superiors. And for women, particularly in the case of someone like Ono-san, there is the possibility that advice from superiors on how to be a more effective leader is doled out in gendered ways that fall within scripted roles for femininity and masculinity.

As a whole, Japanese men think more about culture while Japanese women think more about gender, this distinction reflecting what each group faces as its greatest impediment to achievement of the highest levels of authority at the company. Gender and cultural differences in attitudes toward authority are operant at all levels of Transco, including senior management, but reflect at the higher levels more opaque impediments to the career prospects of men and women that are rooted in issues of trust.

In a company such as Transco, where women not only are promoted with regularity but are also perceived to be, in many instances, a key component of Transco's competitive advantage in Japan, men and women still talk about their world of work in gendered ways, with men much more likely than women to assume a future role of increasing importance for themselves as individual employees. Their sense of importance is threatened by globalization as the company's new take on cultural perspective. Though women are somewhat concerned with globalization, their gender and authority issues remain the same whether or not globalization occurs.

Both gender and culture issues, however, impede understanding of the lines of authority even when the organizational hierarchy is objectively clear. Meetings are often characterized by one or more of these three aspects—gender, culture, and authority—operating at cross-purposes. When meetings occur between people of relatively equal rank, hierarchies based on culture or gender or both often emerge to take the place of an authority figure. When meetings do have a clear authority figure present, culture and gender might either be completely eliminated as a factor for negotiation or greatly exacerbated, depending on the proclivities of the person in authority.

People of American and Japanese nationalities frame cultural and gender distinctions in the workplace, but the expatriated management comprise the majority of people in power. Thus they are under the impression that their ideas hold greater ideological sway in terms of how things should work at the company. While this emphasis is true for many of the concrete ways in which the Japanese employees do their work, it is not true for how the Japanese perceive their work. Gender and culture are contested continually within the issue of workplace authority. Direct contestation is rare, but subtle versions are many. They are seen most clearly in meetings but also are reflected in interviews.

Gender, culture, and authority are factors that mitigate both the internal and external assessment of an individual's contribution, past, present, and future, to the successes and failures of most corporations. The more obvious forms of workplace discrimination have been eliminated in many ways, but truly meritocratic organizations of any kind continue to elude us nonetheless. Especially in the area of promotion to the higher levels of authority in the transnational case studied here, Americans continue to fare better than Japanese, and men of both nationalities still fare better than women in many ways.

As an individual rises on the corporate ladder in any institution, however, the desire for self-reproduction, an institutionalized form of predilection, usually grows stronger. Indeed, in this research "difference" seems to be used increasingly as a weapon in the negative evaluation of employees at the higher levels more so than lower down the hierarchy. Positive and negative difference is defined by the people in power at the top of the corporation. Their attitudes filter down the corporate hierarchy but are reevaluated and reinterpreted along the way. In addition, employees have their own ideas about difference and what types are acceptable or not, within both themselves and other employees. Disagreements as to what constitutes acceptable differences between employees as they attempt to rise up the corporate hierarchy affect self-assessment as well as day-to-day interactions with coworkers.

Cultural differences clash more openly than those of gender. Quests for authority, for example, extend to competition for cultural superiority, most notably in those aspects of culture that are considered essential to the success of the corporation in Japan. These include characteristics of the ideal employee as well as the type of corporate culture most suitable to the greater Japanese environment within which the company is situated.

In terms of gender, gains for women at the lower and middle levels of the corporation mask some of the constraints that remain at the higher levels, where objective criteria carry less weight. Most employees who make it to the uppermost rungs of middle management, whether female or male, have largely matched the objective criteria up to that point, although there are exceptions common to any organization. The increasing tendency toward self-replication at the higher levels encourages a switch to subjective assessment of an individual's abilities. The prospective senior manager is looked at with new eyes. What would he or she be like as a peer? How would subordinates respond to her or him as a leader? Does he or she have the vision to guide the company and the capability to realize the vision? These are nebulous questions that have little basis in objectivity, but they are an essential part of the assessment of one's promotion prospects.

Such questions are attached to the proverbial glass ceiling that divides the middle level from the top level in a corporation. The glass ceiling not only has women looking up; it also has men looking down and deciding who gets to come through, but exactly what they are thinking and why are not clear. In a transnational setting, this same dynamic is also operant along the lines of culture and nationality. Japanese men en route to senior management are evaluated in part on the basis of their cultural inclinations to be more or less traditionally Japanese as defined by senior American management. This pattern parallels gender evaluations of managerial women who often have to negotiate a delicate balance between appearing like a leader without acting like a man.

Japanese men also sometimes choose to use culture as a weapon against their female Japanese coworkers when it appears that the women are faring better at the company in adaptation to the corporate culture. Thus women have to negotiate more constraints than the men. Whereas Japanese of both genders could feel constrained by the senior American management, Japanese women could be also constrained by Japanese men. The transnational corporate setting is characterized by confusion erupting from a number of different directions.

Even when they successfully negotiate cultural conflict at Transco and are viewed by senior managers as likely prospects for promotion to middle management, women's assessments of themselves and their capabilities are confused by the intangibles of male privilege operating underneath the surface. One irony is that Japanese women feel more comfortable with the corporate culture but less able to see a place for themselves in the corporation as a whole, while men are the opposite. Men struggle against the corporate culture because they can envision a place for themselves, while women do not feel a need to struggle against the corporate culture. The culture appears to suit them well even though they feel left out of certain areas.

While men feel more secure as Japanese at the departmental levels, their native culture appears as an obstacle when they consider their future role in the corporation as a whole. Women do not worry as much about their cultural fit with Transco in general but rather their fit with smaller units of operation. Thus, unlike Japanese men, who talk about the corporate culture and conflicts between American and Japanese values, Japanese women talk about the smaller-scale places that women are occupying within the company and use these measures to gauge their own state of affairs.

Because they worry less about their place in the corporation overall, it seems logical that Japanese women clearly would be the ones to expect a future place for themselves in the higher ranks at Transco. While it is true that both Japanese men and women would like to move up in the corporation, the picture is quite complicated and contrary to expectations in many ways.

At least at the time I conducted this research, no attention was given to cultural biases on the part of senior management. The power structure was, however, decidedly non-Japanese, and cultural comparisons became relevant to both Japanese men and senior management. The former engage in constant cultural analysis of the corporation to assess their value as employees, while the latter rely on negative evaluation of certain traits deemed quintessentially Japanese as explanation for why power is yet to be shared more fully.

As people move up in the ranks at Transco, judgment of them and their work becomes less objectively based and more rooted in the subjective assessments of the largely American (white) males in senior management. When negative evaluations are made, for

Japanese men it is primarily on the basis of their lack of "cultural suitability," while for Japanese women, despite the perceived imperative to retain them as a competitive strategy in Japan, it is on the basis of their gender much more than their culture. These same traits of "Japanese-ness" and "female-ness" are never used to explain the basis for positive evaluations.

Predilection for self-replication does become increasingly institutionalized as employees rise on the corporate ladder, and difference of any kind becomes a weapon of negative evaluation by which the dominant structure is able to replicate itself without challenging any of the biases under which it may be operating.[8] It would seem that, beyond special programs for women and lower-level employees, training for senior management specifically designed to improve awareness of personal biases (that stem from acceptance of dominant cultural and gender constructions) is in order. Once promoted to senior management, however, power holders are least likely to take part in any sort of personal development programs. They are, by virtue of being promoted to the highest levels, assumed already to be representative of the corporate ideal, thus reinforcing their tendencies both to self-replicate and to accept the validity of the dominant culture. The time frame required to place larger numbers of any category other than that represented by the current power holders in senior management is thus much longer under the conditions of institutionalized predilection, and calls into question the likelihood of true transnationalism as opposed to cultural and gender dominance posing as cultural integration and gender equity.

Transnationalism, despite its complexity and ambiguous nature, has to be seen as a positive with concrete aims—such as removing binaries that do not really exist outside of our collective mindset. To impose gender and nationality stereotypes on a globalizing organization is to thwart the potential of the transnational, potential that, if realized, would lead to the emergence of the best and brightest across the full spectrum of human resources.

Senior management needs to begin by addressing its own biases. Rather than focusing solely on training and development programs for the multiple categories of employees further down the line, senior managers who truly want to create a merit-based system of reward in the organization need to learn how to model their willingness first to recognize and then to dispense with formulaic approaches to people. We all need further education in how to honor difference without essentializing it—the argument here is certainly not that only senior managers essentialize difference; it is that the essentialisms of senior managers have extremely wide-ranging consequences, and that power has to be recognized and examined in detail.

 Notes

Chapter I

1. For the social sciences, I am availing myself of sociological, anthropological, psychological, economics, and business/organizational studies; for the humanities, I include references to history, philosophy, language, culture, and communication.

2. Whether a corporation should move from a multinational to a transnational form is a matter of debate, but it is not the subject of this research. For a treatment of the pros and cons, however, see Robinson, Dickson, and Knutsen (2007).

3. Theoretically, employees of MNCs who hail from the same country as the parent corporation are more likely to distinguish between their own national culture and any cultures represented by the geographic locations of subsidiaries, seeing their national cultural as "self" and the cultures represented by the subsidiaries as "other." The TNC is supposed to be able to render this self/other distinction meaningless. For a discussion of societal methods of dealing with *otherness* as globalization unfolds, see sociologist Beck (2004). Dwyer (1977, and 1979) offers an earlier but important take on the concepts of *self* and *other* in anthropology.

4. Sources include Boas (1982); Clifford and Marcus (1986); Geertz (1983 and 1973); Samovar and Porter (1999); and Tedlock (1979).

5. Tom Rohlen (1989:5) observes: "Patterns that are broadly isomorphic or historically continuous within a particular society we have generally

labeled cultural. In giving any such pattern this label, however, we imply a form of causality that is not only difficult to untangle and prove, but one that stimulates a conventional set of now all too familiar misunderstandings." These kinds of misunderstandings permeated Transco.

6. Foster (1999) makes a convincing argument that gender theorists and sexual difference theorists use feminist theory in different ways and do not engage in dialogue about the underlying assumptions respective to each; although Foster ultimately finds gender theorizing more analytically useful, she nonetheless makes a call for this dialogue. For an analysis of sameness versus difference with respect to gender, see Wesselius (2000).

7. A variety of interesting works focus on or include the subject of gender as learned behavior, some of which are cited later in this book. Examples include Lorber (1994) and Lorber and Farrell (1991) on gender as a social institution; Alvesson and Billing (1997) on gender and organizations; and Kimmel (2000) on a comprehensive treatment of gender and society.

8. In addition to Valian's (1999) work, a number of studies have shown the difficulties with asserting female authority in the workplace. For examples, see Eagly and Karau (2002); Ridgeway (2001); and Schein (2001).

9. Complete transformation is, according to Martin (1977), a fundamental problem for dominant groups under capitalism.

10. Fine and Buzzanell (2000) analyze the difficulties for women who attempt to exercise leadership, much of which I equate with authority.

11. Examples include Acker (1991); Sorenson (1984).

12. Hochschild (1985) analyzes the "emotion work" required of both men and women in certain jobs that entail contact with the public.

13. An interesting example is Cockburn (1985).

14. As represented in the work of Lenski ([1966] 1984).

15. See M. Adler (1993) for a detailed analysis.

16. Even in family-based capitalism in Japan, wives usually assumed "temporary headship" of the business until a son reached maturity or a daughter married a man willing to take her family name. In this latter case, however, it can be argued that the daughter was still assuming the household headship, "becoming a man in the guise of a woman" (Hamabata 1990:45).

17. Ishida (1993) notes a stronger link in Japan between elite institutions of higher education and the top of the hierarchy of corporate and public organizations, a factor that primarily affects men and remains true in 2008.

18. Fields (1983) first identified the discerning nature of the Japanese female consumer based on his work experiences in Japan; the characterization remains apt.

19. When I returned to Transco in 1999 for additional research, the head of the Japan division had moved his office down several floors from

the top to increase his visibility in the organization. His secretary moved with him.

20. Abe-san's supervisor, however, simply thought that Abe-san added an *o* sound to the end of everything he said. He did not understand that it is common for some Japanese speakers of English to rely on the Japanese syllabary for pronunciation. The syllabary contains roughly fifty sounds that form the basis of the spoken language, almost all of which are constituted from pairing a consonant with a vowel.

21. This article is also available online at http://www.usnews.com/ usnews/biztech/articles/010625/archive_037890.htm.

22. Thomas, Jr. (2007).

Chapter 2

1. Takahashi (1998) notes that in 1960, despite the strong decline in agriculture after World War II, the figures for women working in family businesses versus outside employment were still 43 and 41 percent, respectively, with 70 percent of women's employment in family businesses located in the primary sector (such as agriculture and fisheries).

2. Sources include Economic Planning Agency (1997).

3. There are numerous sources for this datum, including Sugimoto (1997); Takahashi (1998).

4. The percentage of women in the total workforce in 2005 was 41 percent, up from 37 percent in 1980, with the biggest increase during the 1990s. During this so-called lost decade, more women were hired as a way to lower costs during the economic crisis. The 50 percent figure refers to the percentage of all women who are employed, whether part-time or not. In 2007, Japan boasted eight million part-time workers, more than 90 percent of whom were women. See Faiola (2007).

5. The fundamentals of the successful Japanese corporation listed by Abegglen and Stalk (1985:5) were reinforced by many academic studies of the time period.

6. For example, see Tomita (1991).

7. Imai and Itami (1988) argue the case most eloquently and briefly.

8. The use of the term *part-time* is a misnomer in Japan given that it includes any employment that requires up to 35 hours per week.

9. Rohlen (1979) was one of the few scholars to mention this fact at the time.

10. See the newspaper article by Faiola (2007).

11. Koike (1988) refers to the "permanent employment" and "seniority wages" characterizations of Japanese industry as a distorted view based on a culturalist interpretation of Japan as unique, noting that many parallels exist

in American industry and that these features in Japan are limited primarily to very large companies. However, even in this view, the beneficiaries are still white- and blue-collar men. See also Hamada (1992, 1980); Noguchi (1990); Plath (1983); and Skinner (1983).

12. Japan Ministry of Labor (1988); Lam (1992).

13. Ogasawara (1998:21) lists the figures for *kakarichō* (chief) in 1995 as 6 to 9 percent, depending on the size of the company.

14. Exact figures are difficult to come by but currently hover around 3 percent. Ogasawara (1998:19) gives 1 percent as the figure for 1995, which includes both company managers and government officials.

15. The survey of large- and medium-sized enterprises was conducted by the Japan Institute of Workers' Evolution, as presented in Sakata (2007).

16. Haley (1991) is one example, but this view of the government is widespread.

17. The EEOL was amended in 1997 (effective 1999) to include a *mandatory* ban on discrimination in recruitment, job assignment, and promotion; it also ends special treatment of women in limits placed on overtime, allows for government arbitration of individual complaints, orders the publication of the names of companies who fail to comply, and addresses sexual harassment (Takahashi 1998). It remained ineffective and was revised again in 2007 to include much stricter enforcement of compliance and consideration of gender equality as opposed to women's equality (Gross and Minot 2007). It is still too early to know what effects these latest amendments will have on career women's employment. See Mikanagi (2000) for an analysis of how and why the Japanese state promotes gender inequality in the labor force.

18. Kawashima (1995) outlines both the history of Japanese working women and the effects of the first phase of the EEOL.

19. N. Adler (1993).

20. Hasegawa (1986) is but one example of this popular view.

21. Ibid.

22. See Jung and Cheon (2006) for a comparison of employment practices in Korea and Japan after the Asian economic crisis of the late 1990s; on the growth of nonstandard work in postbubble Japan, see Houseman and Osawa (2003) and Nagase (2003).

23. Ikeuchi (1988) shows the effects of the aging workforce in Japan, but in 2008, the costs of hiring women were still being weighed.

24. Lam (1992).

25. Beck and Beck (1994). Job-hopping has become even more popular in recent years.

26. Huddleston (1990).

27. Tanaka (1995).

28. Although many people argue that Japanese women prefer to work part-time as a supplement to their primary duties in the home, or to avoid income tax penalties, the definition of *part-time work* as up to 35 hours per week means that women work nearly full time without receiving benefits.

29. Again, the figure for part-time workers in 2007 was 8 million, 90 percent of whom are women (Faiola 2007).

30. Takahashi (1998:7), citing Ootsubo (1998).

31. Japan Ministry of Labor (1998); Shuukan Diamondo (1998); Takahashi (1998).

32. Adler (1987).

33. Saso (1990).

34. Saso (1990).

35. Ide, in Buckley (1997).

36. Endo (1995).

37. Based on data from Japan Ministry of Labor (1993); Kawashima (1995); Ogasawara (1998); and Sakata (2007).

38. Kawashima (1995).

39. Zimmeck (1992); Martin (1991).

40. Ramsay and Parker (1992).

41. Boyd (1990).

42. Kanter (1977).

43. For a feminist approach to socialization in organizations, see Bullis and Stout (2000).

44. Kanter (1977); Kleinman (1996); Reskin and Padavic (1994); Schroedel (1985); Segura (1992); Williams (2000).

45. Bergmann (1986); Reskin and Padavic (1994).

46. Hall (1984); Hall and Halberstadt (1986).

47. Hochschild (1985).

48. See DeWitt (1995).

49. Kristen B. Frasch, "Few Women Climbing to the Top," *Human Resources Executive Online,* March 17, 2008, http://www.hreonline.com/HRE/story.jsp?storyId=80326347.

50. Two additional points are worth noting: (1) male vestiges of power persist below the glass ceiling for technologically oriented, high-paying occupations; and (2) within the range of working class occupations, one can witness a microcosm of the overall occupational hierarchy of gender, with working class men dominating the top end.

51. The Japanese women's assessments of both American and Japanese companies were neither unrealistic nor particularly accurate. For example, in terms of entrance to avenues of authority, we can probably rule out differences in human capital as the sole explanation for discrimination against women in much the same way that these differences have been

challenged to explain fully the discrimination in employment opportunities. Numerous studies of the latter have shown, even after accounting for an ever-increasing number of human capital variables, the persistence of a residual, thought to be evidence of some type of discrimination rooted in "cultural" factors (Blau and Ferber 1992; de Miranda 1994). Education, an important variable in the type of occupation one will hold as well as the salary one can command, has a positive effect for women, with the notable exception of Japan, but falls far short of its expected effects as a gender equalizer (de Miranda 1994; Ram 1982; Strober 1990) even in non-Japanese contexts.

This same type of residual of discrimination appears also to block women's access to the higher managerial levels of employment. Variations in human capital attributes do not explain gender differences in workplace authority (Jaffee 1989, for example). And Wright, Baxter, and Birkleund's (1995) survey of the gender gap in workplace authority (GGWA) found considerable cross-national variation—of the seven target countries, the GGWA was lowest in the United States and highest in Japan—but the pattern of variation did not appear to be the result of gender differences in personal attributes, employment settings, or self-selection. It was concluded that the GGWA is most fully explained by a causal relationship between the availability of managerial positions and the political capacity of women's movements to challenge barriers to assumption of authority positions. This factor would account for Japanese women being behind American women in workplace advancement. It also makes the case that many corporations are reluctant to promote women to the highest levels (or even middle levels in Japan) unless forced to do so.

52. I do not have data on Transco's compensation packages, but a number of women believed that their pay was very generous and, in fact, a disadvantage when it came to finding a spouse as the potential suitor might be threatened by the women's salary. Women's wages in Japanese corporations are substantially lower than men's, with high levels of gender stratification in the workforce as a compounding factor. See Aiba and Wharton (2001) and Brinton (1988, 1989, 1993).

53. For a general treatment of feminism in Japan, see Buckley (1997), as well as Fujimura-Fanselow and Kameda (1995), which includes the historical underpinnings.

54. It is important to note that the upper limit on the age of marriage continues to rise for both men and women, as it has for some time. What is new since the time of this research, however, is the increase in the numbers of women who are single by choice; these include the so-called parasite singles (women who remain in residence with their parents) as well as those who live on their own.

55. White (1993).

56. In addition to care of children, wives often are expected to be the primary caretakers of elderly parents as social services for seniors in Japan are quite limited. For an interesting look at motherhood or wifedom in Japan, see Allison (1996), Borovoy (2005), Fujimura-Fanselow and Kameda (1994), Fujita (1989), and Ueno (1994); for comparisons across countries, see Fuwa (2004).

57. Kingston (2004) describes a variety of gender changes in Japan, including the decline in women's interest in marriage. While not disputing this trend, most of the women in my study claimed to have a desire to marry.

Chapter 3

1. See Thompson's (1967) widely-read analysis of complex organizations and rational behavior.

2. For example, Odaka (1986). Note that *groupism* has rightly come under fire as a gross over-generalization of social life in Japan, but the company-as-family metaphor remains an apt description of many Japanese corporations, especially the large ones.

3. See descriptions in Abegglen and Stalk (1985), Baba et al. (1983), Dore (1973), and Rohlen (1974).

4. Lam (1992) provides an interesting analysis of this disruption.

5. An example of this argument appeared in "Shokuba wa kawatta ka" *Asahi Shinbun,* October 18–22, 1995.

6. Kathleen S. Uno (1993) argues that the late-nineteenth-century, government-promoted concept of the "good wife, wise mother" (*ryōsai kenbo*) remains influential in postwar Japan, with the continuation of an emphasis on motherhood over wifehood that began before the war to address the state's childbearing concerns. We can see recent evidence of the state's conflicting attitudes toward women in Health Minister Yanagisawa's reference to Japanese women as "baby-making machines." Among others, see "In Japan, A Revolution over Childbearing," *Time,* February 5, 2007.

7. Lebra (1984) refers to "anticipatory socialization" of females who become professionals. The family plays a crucial role in this process, especially the father.

8. Fields (1983); he also notes that Japanese housewives are a very powerful consumer group.

9. McVeigh (1997) describes the interesting combination of femininity and internationalization that characterizes women's junior colleges.

10. According to Peak (1991), preschool in Japan sets the stage for learning the value of group life; however, both preschool and primary school are considerably less strict than middle and high school.

11. For a fascinating comparison of the teen years and socialization in Japan and the United States, see White (1993); her treatment of education in Japan (1987) is also well worth reading.

12. For a thorough treatment of women's difficulties in obtaining good career opportunities even as graduates of top universities in Japan and the United States, see Strober and Chan (1999).

Chapter 4

1. Rather than being motivated by personal discriminatory thinking per se, employers are motivated by the need to maximize profits. Decisions about hiring and promotion entail risks because it is not possible to know fully how well an individual employee will perform on the job. Thus employers rely on commonly held beliefs about the productivity of certain groups, and men are commonly believed to be more productive than women. The result is discrimination against individual employees. See Aigner and Cain (1977); Arrow (1972, 1977); Phelps (1972).

2. And if we follow the recommendations of Jean Hollands' program for women executives called "Bully Broads," even successful (as in profit-making) female executives need to learn to behave differently than their male counterparts. Although it seems that the title of this program, which generated a lot of media attention in the early 1990s, is no longer in use, many of the same dictates of the program can be found in Hollands book (see Hollands (2002) in References for one version of the reprints) and in the current (2008) programs offered by the Growth and Leadership Center that Hollands founded in 1980 (see www.glcweb.com for more information). These programs promote many of the gender stereotypes that I argue serve ultimately to place more rather than fewer limitations on both men's and women's capacity for managerial success. See Chapter 4 for more details on the "Bully Broads" program.

3. Parts of Valian's argument are similar to those made by Kimmel (2000) as presented in Chapter 1.

4. In addition to Kanter's (1977) work on social homogeneity in the corporation, Useem (1984) analyzes a similar phenomenon in the rise of business politics.

5. For a detailed treatment of the generally prescriptive nature of women's magazines in Japan, see Tanaka (1998).

6. DiMaggio (1997) provides additional insight as to the ways in which culture works through information distribution, mental structures, and symbolic systems.

7. See Lorber (1994), and Lorber and Farrell (1991).

8. See the chapter by West and Zimmerman in Lorber and Farrell (1991).

9. Connell (1988) provides eloquent theorizing on the shifting nature of gender.

10. See Connell (1987, 1988).

11. Studies of how gender operates in the workplace include Game and Pringle (1983), and O'Donnell (1984).

12. Williams (2000) provides evidence for the saliency of masculine norms in various characterizations of the ideal worker.

13. See Morrison, White, and Velsor (1987, 1994).

14. See Goffman (1963) on the nature of stigma, and see Kusow's (2004) analysis of this work. Even without stigma in the organization, Milligan (2003:381) states that "displacement leads to identity discontinuity and that nostalgia provides one way of maintaining or regaining identity continuity." She is referring to displacement by means of physical relocation, but I think a similar connection can be made to feelings of identity discontinuity as a result of nationality displacement.

15. For a thorough treatment of Japanese women's language, see Ide (1979); Inoue (2002); and Shibamoto (1985).

16. The dual-persona pattern also reflects the idea of the *kanjin*, the "contextual person" in Japanese scholarship. See Henshall (1999).

17. For a critical analysis of the problems that occur when women from rich countries hire domestic help, especially in the form of women from poor countries who must leave their own children behind, to solve their second shift burdens, see Parreñas (2001).

18. In 2008 I also learned from one contact that the imported program is no longer in use at Transco.

Chapter 5

1. In terms of the value of authority as an organizing principle of the Japanese corporation, however, the principle of *wa* (harmony) mitigates the concept of authority as hierarchical directives. The continued use of the *ringi* system of decision making (Ballon 1969; Brown 1966), in which all participants in a decision sign a memorandum that summarizes the decision, as well as the considerable *nemawashi* (literally, "digging around the root," it refers to extensive discussion and solicitation of views) that takes place prior to the making of the actual decision itself (Abegglen and Stalk 1985), marks work relationships as more collective and consensual (Clark 1979). Supervisor and subordinate are likely to work side by side and be engaged in constant conversation, leading to the speculation that information of all

kinds, including advice (and criticism in very informal instances) flows more freely from the Japanese (than the Western) subordinate (Nevins 1988). This style may make it more difficult for women managers of a native Japanese corporation, given the appearance of greater discomfort with cross-gender work relations when the parties are of equal employment status, but it is also possible that this type of relational management is more suited to women.

2. Shils ([1994] 2001) is an example.

3. For example, see Goldthorpe and Hope (1972).

4. See a 1977 study by Treiman that included Japan and Taiwan.

5. Webb (1984) demonstrates the nuance that gender analysis can lend to studies of deference and authority.

6. Bayes (1978) is one example.

7. Examples include Kondo (1990) and Smith (1992).

8. This is the conclusion of Bayes (1978).

9. Again, the paradox here is that possessing the traits ascribed to women would have denied Ono-san's legitimation as an authority figure. See Tretheway (2000).

10. The lone exception on the Japanese side was a male who worked in what was considered to be the most aggressive product category in terms of its own subculture within the company. As reported to me by a number of people, this category has a long history of male domination in its employee ranks and a culture that is best characterized by metaphors of war. An example of a meeting between this group and Walter, the head of Transco, appears later in this chapter.

11. Rohlen (1975) provides a lively description of this phenomenon.

12. As mentioned in the notes to Chapter 4, the "Bully Broads" program seems to have ended, but the center that offered the program has replaced it with several programs that promote many of the same ideas as those in the "Bully Broads" program.

13. Hofstede's (1997) study of differences between societal cultures and the attendant effects on organizations focuses in part on the feminine-masculine vector. On this dimension, Hofstede defines the characteristics of the masculine side as valuing an opportunity for both high earnings and advancement, getting personal recognition for doing a good job, and being challenged on the job such that one gains a sense of personal accomplishment; for the feminine side, the values are a good relationship with one's boss, cooperative relationships with coworkers, living in a desirable area, and job security (pp. 81–82). He goes on to specify differences in behavior based on these values: *Masculinity* "stands for a society in which emotional gender roles are clearly distinct: men are supposed to be assertive, tough, and focused on material success; women are supposed to be more modest,

tender, and concerned with the quality of life"; *femininity* stands for a society in which emotional gender roles overlap: both men and women are supposed to be modest, tender, and concerned with the quality of life" (pp. 401–402). Hofstede computes via factor analysis the location of fifty countries (and three regions) on a masculinity index, with 0 as the most feminine and 100 as the most masculine (in itself perhaps a gender statement). Japan scores the highest of all, with a 95, while the United States scores a 62, still on the masculine side but less so (Scandinavian countries and the Netherlands are the most feminine, all with scores of 16 and below).

14. For general examples of gender socialization, see Oskamp and Constanzo (1993); Renzetti and Curran (1989); and Stevenson (1994). For cultural manifestations of gender differences, see Etaugh and Bridges (2000). For gender socialization in schools, see Lloyd and Duveen (1993); Sadker and Sadker (1994). For gender as a social process that divides children in schools, see Thorne (1993).

15. For another analysis of female expertise and male authority, see Savage (1992).

Chapter 6

1. Hooper (2000) argues that globalization highlights awareness of multiple masculinities, which for the purposes of my research may provide one way for senior male management to begin to understand their differences from one another.

2. I have not directly corroborated the updates with each of the six subjects; I am reporting what I was told about all six people by two of the subjects and the updates they provided me were the same for each subject.

3. Learning a foreign language helps to disrupt the thought patterns that are continually reinforced in one's native language. In this sense, the Japanese employees at Transco have a leg up on the American management, who study Japanese at most for three hours per week and remain functionally illiterate in the language. The Japanese employees who are bilingual have a larger lens through which to view the overall picture. However, I do not wish to say that transnationalism *requires* bilingual or trilingual abilities but merely to point out that those abilities might be able to counter certain mindsets that are anathema to transnational thinking. In the conditions of a transnational corporation that has a plan similar to Transco's parent corporation, where employees are expected to be able to move around global operations in a relatively seamless way, there has to be some semblance of a *lingua franca*. In this case, as in so many, it is English. Thus, on the one hand, I am recommending expanding language capabilities—if one is going to live in Japan working at Transco for several years, why not learn the language and

have all the benefits that come with that, many of which go well beyond language—but on the other hand, accepting the necessity of a *lingua franca* and examining how transnational thinking might occur nonetheless.

4. I am indebted to the work of Waller and Marcos (2005) for some of my thinking on the need to incorporate difference more effectively if paradigmatic changes are to be made, whether in feminist theory as is the subject of their work or in human relations at the level of the transnational corporation.

5. For a treatment of chaos theory in regard to the increase in uncertainty as our world becomes more complex, see Merry (1995). For a text that includes chaos theory as it takes the reader on multiple intellectual rides that are described accurately in the foreword as "wild," see de Rosnay (2000). Other suggested readings on chaos theory include Polley (1997), Reuther and Fairhurst (2000), and Thiétart and Forgues (1995).

6. An article on the increase in the divorce rate after Japan enacted a new law in 2007 that entitles a spouse to up to half of her husband's pension also noted: "In 1980, about three-quarters of Japan's college-educated women were married by age 29. Now, seven out of 10 are single at that age. In the past 20 years, the percentage of women in this elite demographic category who do not want to marry at all has almost doubled—to about 29 percent." (Harden 2007: A01).

7. Blair-Loy (2001) provides some examples of both the progress and the struggles for women in management.

8. To quote Olthuis (2000:4) in a passage that refers to modernity, but which I think also applies well to any dominant structure: "Masquerading as the universal deliverances of reason which as such are considered self-evident, personal and particular stances can become enshrined in institutional and cultural practices as 'neutral' and 'normal,' even if they are actually discriminatory and oppressive to those of competing or differing allegiances."

References

Abegglen, James C., and George Stalk, Jr. 1985. *Kaisha, The Japanese Corporation.* New York: Basic Books.

Acker, Joan. 1991. "Hierarchies, Jobs, Bodies: A Theory of Gendered Organizations." Pp. 162–179 in *The Social Construction of Gender,* edited by J. Lorber and S. Farrell. Newbury Park, CA: Sage Publications.

Adler, Mariana. 1993. "Gender Differences in Job Autonomy: The Consequences of Occupational Segregation and Authority Position." *Sociological Quarterly* 34:449–465.

Adler, Nancy J. 1987. "Pacific Basin Managers: A Gaijin, Not a Woman." *Human Resource Management* 26:169–191.

———. 1993. "Asian Women in Management." *International Studies of Management and Organization* 23:3–17.

Aiba, Keiko, and Amy S. Wharton. 2001. "Job-Level Sex Composition and the Sex Pay Gap in a Large Japanese Firm." *Sociological Perspectives* 44:67–87.

Aigner, Dennis J., and Glen G. Cain. 1977. "Statistical Theories of Discrimination in Labor Markets." *Industrial and Labor Relations Review* 30:175–187.

Allinson, Gary D. 1997. *Japan's Postwar History.* Ithaca, NY: Cornell University Press.

Allison, Anne. 1996. "Producing Mothers." Pp. 135–155 in *Re-imaging Japanese Women,* edited by A. E. Imamura. Berkeley: University of California Press.

Alvesson, Mats, and Yvonne Due Billing. 1997. *Understanding Gender and Organizations*. London: Sage Publications.

Aron, Raymond. 1988. *Power, Modernity, and Sociology*. Hants, U.K.: Edward Elgar.

Arrow, Kenneth J. 1972. "Models of Job Discrimination." Pp. 83–102 in *Racial Discrimination in Economic Life*, edited by A. H. Pascal. Lexington, MA: Lexington Books.

———. 1977. "The Theory of Discrimination." *Industrial and Labor Relations Review* 30:175–187.

Asahi Shinbun. 1995. "Shokuba wa kawatta ka." October 18–22.

Baba, Masao, R. Perloff, F. Baba, M. Lewis, and H. Iwade. 1983. *A Comparative Survey on the Managerial Climate in the U.S. and Japanese Business Organization*. Tokyo: Nihon University, College of Economics, Institute of Industrial Management Research.

Ballon, R. J. 1969. "The Japanese Dimensions of Industrial Enterprises." Pp. 3–40 in *The Japanese Employee*, edited by R. J. Ballon. Tokyo: Sophia University.

Bannerjee, Neela. 2001. "Some 'Bullies' Seek Ways to Soften Up; Toughness Has Risks for Women Executives." *New York Times*, August 10, C1.

Bayes, Marjorie. 1978. "Women in Authority: A Sociopsychological Analysis." *Journal of Applied Behavioral Science* 14:7–20.

Beck, John C., and Martha N. Beck. 1994. *The Change of a Lifetime: Employment Patterns among Japan's Managerial Elite*. Honolulu: University of Hawaii Press.

Beck, Ulrich. 2004. "The Truth of Others: A Cosmopolitan Approach." *Common Knowledge* 10:430–449.

Becker, Howard S. 2003. "The Politics of Presentation: Goffman and Total Institutions." *Symbolic Interaction* 26:659–669.

Bergmann, Barbara R. 1986. *The Economic Emergence of Women*. New York: Basic Books.

Bielby, William T., and James N. Baron. 1986. "Men and Women at Work: Sex Segregation and Statistical Discrimination." *American Journal of Sociology* 91:759–799.

Blair-Loy, Mary. 2001. "It's Not Just What You Know, It's Who You Know: Technical Knowledge, Rainmaking, and Gender among Finance Executives." *Research in the Sociology of Work* 10:51–83.

Blau, Francine D., and Marianne A. Ferber. 1992. *The Economics of Women, Men, and Work*. Englewood Cliffs, NJ: Prentice Hall.

Boas, Franz. 1982. *Race, Language, and Culture*. Chicago: University of Chicago Press.

Borovoy, Amy. 2005. *The Too-Good Wife: Alcohol, Codependency, and the Politics of Nurturance in Postwar Japan*. Berkeley: University of California Press.

Bourdieu, Pierre. 1977. *Outline of a Theory of Practice*. Cambridge: Cambridge University Press.

———. 1990. *The Logic of Practice*. Stanford, CA: Stanford University Press.

Boyd, Monica. 1990. *Patriarchy and Postindustrialism:Women and Power in the Service Economy*. New Haven, CT:Yale University Press.

Brinton, Mary C. 1988. "The Social-Institutional Bases of Gender Stratification: Japan as an Illustrative Case." *American Journal of Sociology* 94:300–334.

———. 1989. "Gender Stratification in Contemporary Urban Japan." *American Sociological Review* 54:549–564.

———. 1993. *Women and the Economic Miracle: Gender and Work in Postwar Japan*. Berkeley: University of California Press.

Brown, W. 1966. "Japanese Management:The Cultural Background." *Monumenta Nipponica* 21:47–60.

Buckley, Sandra. 1997. *Broken Silence:Voices of Japanese Feminism*. Berkeley: University of California Press.

Bullis, Connie, and Karen Rohrbauck Stout. 2000. "Organizational Socialization: A Feminist Standpoint Approach." Pp. 47–75 in *Rethinking Organizational and Managerial Communication from Feminist Perspectives*, edited by Patrice M. Buzzanell. Thousand Oaks, CA: Sage Publications.

Chang, Johannes Han-Yin. 2004. "Mead's Theory of Emergence as a Framework for Multilevel Sociological Inquiry." *Symbolic Interaction* 27:405–427.

Clark, Rodney. 1979. *The Japanese Company*. New Haven, CT:Yale University Press.

Clifford, James, and George E. Marcus (Eds.). 1986. *Writing Culture: The Poetics and Politics of Ethnography*. Berkeley: University of California Press.

Cockburn, Cynthia. 1985. *Machinery of Dominance:Women, Men, and Technical Know-How*. London: Pluto Press.

Connell, R. W. 1987. *Gender and Power: Society, the Person, and Sexual Politics*. Cambridge, U.K.: Polity Press.

———. 1988. *Gender as a Structure of Power*. Sydney: George Allen and Unwin.

de Miranda, G. V. 1994. "Education and Female Labor Force Participation in Industrializing Countries." Pp. 1666–1672 in *The International Encyclopedia of Education*. New York: Pergamon Press.

de Rosnay, Joël. 2000. *The Symbiotic Man:A New Understanding of the Organization of Life and a Vision of the Future*. New York: McGraw-Hill.

DeWitt, Karen. 1995. "Panel's Study Cites Job Bias for Minorities and Women," *New York Times*, November 23.

DiMaggio, Paul. 1997. "Culture and Cognition." *Annual Review of Sociology.* 23:263–287.

Dore, Ronald. 1973. *British Factory–Japanese Factory:The Origins of National Diversity in Industrial Relations.* Berkeley: University of California Press.

Dwyer, Kevin. 1977. "On the Dialogic of Field Work." *Dialectical Anthropology* 2:143–151.

———. 1979. "The Dialogic of Ethnology." *Dialectical Anthropology* 4: 205–224.

Eagly, Alice H., and Steven J. Karau. 2002. "Role Congruity Theory of Prejudice toward Female Leaders." *Psychological Review* 109:573–598.

Economic Planning Agency. 1997. *Heisei 9 nen ban Kokumin Seikatsu Hakusho.* Tokyo: Ministry of Finance.

Economist. 2001. "The Wrong Trousers." June 16–22, p.68

Endo, Orie. 1995. "Aspects of Sexism in Language." Pp. 29–42 in *Japanese Women: New Feminist Perspectives on the Past, Present, and Future,* edited by K. Fujimura-Fanselow and A. Kameda. New York: Feminist Press, City University of New York.

Etaugh, Claire A., and Judith S. Bridges. 2000. *The Psychology of Women: A Lifespan Perspective.* New York: Pearson Education.

Faiola, Anthony. 2007. "Japanese Working Women Still Serve the Tea," *Washington Post,* March 2, A09.

Fields, George. 1983. *From Bonsai to Levi's.* New York: Mentor.

Fine, Marlene G., and Patrice M. Buzzanell. 2000. "Walking the High Wire: Leadership Theorizing, Daily Acts, and Tensions." Pp. 128–156 in *Rethinking Organizational and Managerial Communication from Feminist Perspectives,* edited by Patrice M. Buzzanell. Thousand Oaks, CA: Sage Publications.

Foster, Johanna. 1999. "An Invitation to Dialogue: Clarifying the Position of Feminist Gender Theory in Relation to Sexual Difference Theory." *Gender & Society* 13:431–456.

Frasch, Kristen B. 2008. "Few Women Climb to the Top." *Human Resources Executive Online.* March 17. http://www.hreonline.com/HRE/story.jsp ?storyId=80326347.

Freidson, Eliot. 1983. "Celebrating Erving Goffman, 1983." *Contemporary Sociology* 12:359–362.

Fujimura-Fanselow, Kumiko, and Atsuko Kameda. 1994. "Women's Education and Gender Roles in Japan." Pp. 43–68 in *Women of Japan and Korea: Continuity and Change,* edited by J. Gelb and M. L. Palley. Philadelphia: Temple University Press.

———. (Eds.). 1995. *Japanese Women: New Feminist Perspectives on the Past, Present, and Future.* New York: Feminist Press, City University of New York.

Fujita, Mariko. 1989. "It's All Mother's Fault: Childcare and the Socialization of Working Mothers in Japan." *Journal of Japanese Studies* 15:67–91.

Fuwa, Makiko. 2004. "Macro-Level Gender Inequality and the Division of Household Labor in 22 Countries." *American Sociological Review* 69:751–767.

Game, Ann, and Rosemary Pringle. 1983. *Gender at Work*. Sydney: George Allen and Unwin.

Geertz, Clifford. 1973. *The Interpretation of Cultures*. New York: Basic Books.

———. 1983. *Local Knowledge: Further Essays in Interpretive Anthropology*. New York: Basic Books.

Giddens, Anthony. 1984. *The Constitution of Society: Outline of a Theory of Structuration*. Berkeley: University of California Press.

Goffman, Erving. 1959. *The Presentation of Self in Everyday Life*. London: Doubleday.

———. 1963. *Stigma: Notes on the Management of Spoiled Identities*. Englewood Cliffs, NJ: Prentice Hall.

Goldthorpe, John H., and Keith Hope. 1972. "Occupational Grading and Occupational Prestige." Pp. 23–79 in *The Analysis of Social Mobility: Methods and Approaches*, edited by K. Hope. Oxford: Oxford University Press.

Gross, Arnes, and John Minot. 2007. "The Strengthening of the Toothless Lion: Japan's New Gender Equity Law." Published on HR.com, November. Accessed at http://www.pacificbridge.com/publication.asp?id=102.

Haley, John O. 1991. *Authority without Power: Law and the Japanese Paradox*. New York: Oxford University Press.

Hall, Judith A. 1984. *Nonverbal Sex Differences: Communication Accuracy and Expressive Styles*. Baltimore: Johns Hopkins University Press.

Hall, Judith A., and Amy G. Halberstadt. 1986. "Smiling and Gazing." Pp. 136–158 in *The Psychology of Gender:Advances through Meta-Analysis*, edited by J. Hyde and M. Linn. Baltimore: Johns Hopkins University Press.

Hamabata, Matthews Masayuki. 1990. *Crested Kimono: Power and Love in the Japanese Business Family*. Ithaca, NY: Cornell University Press.

Hamada, Tomoko. 1980. "Winds of Change: Economic Realism and Japanese Labor Management." *Asian Survey* 20:397–406.

———. 1992. "Under the Silk Banner: The Japanese Company and Its Overseas Managers." Pp. 135–164 in *Japanese Social Organization*, edited by T. S. Lebra. Honolulu: University of Hawaii Press.

Harden, Blaine. 2007. "Learn to Be Nice to Your Wife, or Pay the Price." *Washington Post*, November 6, A01.

Hasegawa, Keitaro. 1986. *Japanese-Style Management*. New York: Kodansha International.

Henshall, Kenneth G. 1999. *Dimensions of Japanese Society: Gender, Margins, and Mainstream.* New York: St. Martin's Press.

Hochschild, Arlie. 1985. *The Managed Heart.* Berkeley: University of California Press.

———. 1989. *The Second Shift.* New York: Viking.

Hochschild, Arlie, and Anne Machung. 2003. *The Second Shift.* New York: Penguin.

Hofstede, Geert. 1997. *Cultures and Organizations: Software of the Mind.* New York: McGraw-Hill.

Hollands, Jean. 2002. *Same Game Different Rules: How to Get Ahead Without Being a Bully Broad, Ice Queen, or "Ms. Understood."* New York: McGraw-Hill.

Hooper, Charlotte. 2000. "Masculinities in Transition: The Case of Globalization." Pp. 59–73 in *Gender and Global Restructuring*, edited by Marianne H. Marchand and Anne Sisson Runyan. London: Routledge.

Houseman, Susan, and Machiko Osawa. 2003. "The Growth of Nonstandard Employment in Japan and the United States." Pp. 175–214 in *Nonstandard Work in Developed Economies: Causes and Consequences*, edited by Susan N. Houseman. Kalamazoo, MI: W. E. Upjohn Institute for Employment Research.

Huddleston, Jackson N., Jr. 1990. *Gaijin Kaisha: Running a Foreign Business in Japan.* Armonk, NY: M. E. Sharpe.

Huen, Yuki W. P. 2007. "Workplace Sexual Harassment in Japan: A Review of Combating Measures Taken." *Asian Survey* 47: 811–827.

Ide, Sachiko. 1979. *Onna no Kotoba. Otoko no Kotoba.* Tokyo: Nihon Keizai Tsushinsha.

Ikeuchi, Masato. 1988. "The Impact of Aging." Pp. 231–233 in *Inside the Japanese System*, edited by D. I. Okimoto and T. P. Rohlen. Stanford, CA: Stanford University Press.

Imai, Ken'ichi, and Hiroyuki Itami. 1988. "Allocation of Labor and Capital in Japan and the United States." Pp. 112–118 in *Inside the Japanese System*, edited by D. I. Okimoto and T. P. Rohlen. Stanford, CA: Stanford University Press.

Inoue, Miyako. 2002. "Gender, Language, and Modernity: Toward an Effective History of Japanese Women's Language." *American Ethnologist* 29:392–422.

Ishida, Hiroshi. 1993. *Social Mobility in Contemporary Japan.* Stanford, CA: Stanford University Press.

Jaffee, David. 1989. "Gender Inequality in Workplace Autonomy and Authority." *Social Science Quarterly* 70:375–390.

Japan Ministry of Labor. 1988a. Fujin rōdō no jitsujō. Tokyo: Japan Ministry of Labor.

———. 1988b. Koreika nado shita de no Jinji seido ni kansuru Senmon Iinkai Hokokusho. Tokyo: Japan Ministry of Labor.

———. 1993. Joshi koyo kanri kihon chosa. Tokyo: Japan Ministry of Labor.

———. 1998. Heisei 9 nen ban Hatarau Josei no jitsujō. Tokyo: Japan Ministry of Labor.

Jenkins, Richard. [1992] 2002. *Pierre Bourdieu*. London: Routledge.

Jung, EeHwan, and Byung-you Cheon. 2006. "Economic Crisis and Changes in Employment Relations in Japan and Korea." *Asian Survey* 46:457–476.

Kanter, Rosabeth Moss. 1977. *Men and Women of the Corporation*. New York: Basic Books.

Kawashima, Yoko. 1995. "Female Workers: An Overview of Past and Current Trends." Pp. 271–293 in *Japanese Women: New Feminist Perspectives on the Past, Present, and Future*, edited by K. Fujimura-Fanselow and A. Kameda. New York: Feminist Press, City University of New York.

Kimmel, Michael S. 2000. *The Gendered Society*. New York: Oxford University Press.

Kingston, Jeff. 2004. *Japan's Quiet Transformation: Social Change and Civil Society in the Twenty-first Century*. New York: RoutledgeCurzon.

Kleinman, Sherryl. 1996. *Opposing Ambitions: Gender and Identity in an Alternative Organization*. Chicago: University of Chicago Press.

Koike, Kazuo. 1988. *Understanding Industrial Relations in Modern Japan*. New York: St. Martin's Press.

Kondo, Dorinne K. 1990. *Crafting Selves: Power, Gender, and Discourses of Identity in a Japanese Workplace*. Chicago: University of Chicago Press.

Kunda, Gideon. 1992. *Engineering Culture*. Philadelphia: Temple University Press.

Kusow, Abdi M. 2004. "Contesting Stigma: On Goffman's Assumptions of Normative Order." *Symbolic Interaction* 27:179–197.

Lam, Alice C. L. 1992. *Women and Japanese Management: Discrimination and Reform*. New York: Routledge.

Lebra, Takie Sugiyama. 1984. *Japanese Women: Constraint and Fulfillment*. Honolulu: University of Hawaii Press.

Lenski, Gerhard E. [1966] 1984. *Power and Privilege*. Chapel Hill: University of North Carolina Press.

Lincoln, James R., and Arne L. Kalleberg. 1990. *Culture, Control, and Commitment: A Study of Work Organization and Work Attitudes in the United States and Japan*. Cambridge: Cambridge University Press.

Lloyd, Barbara B., and Gerard Duveen. 1993. *Gender Identities and Education: The Impact of Starting School*. New York: St. Martin's Press.

Lorber, Judith. 1994. *Paradoxes of Gender*. New Haven, CT: Yale University Press.

Lorber, Judith, and Susan A. Farrell (Eds.). 1991. *The Social Construction of Gender.* Newbury Park: Sage Publications.

Martin, Joanne. 1992. *Cultures in Organizations: Three Perspectives.* New York: Oxford University Press.

Martin, Patricia Yancey. 1991. *Gender, Interaction, and Inequality in Organizations.* Tallahassee: Florida State University Press.

Martin, Roderick. 1977. *The Sociology of Power.* London: Routledge & Kegan Paul.

Maynard, Senko K. 1997. *Japanese Communication: Language and Thought in Context.* Honolulu: University of Hawaii Press.

McDonald, Marci. 2001. "Lingerie's Iron Maiden Undone: Linda Wachner, the Latest CEO in Trouble." *U.S. News and World Report,* June 25, 37.

McVeigh, Brian J. 1997. *Life in a Japanese Women's College: Learning to Be Ladylike.* London: Nissan Institute/Routledge.

Mead, George Herbert. 1934. *Mind, Self, and Society.* Chicago: University of Chicago Press.

Merry, Uri. 1995. *Coping with Uncertainty: Insights from the New Sciences of Chaos, Self-organization, and Complexity.* Westport, CT: Praeger Publishers.

Mikanagi, Yumiko. 2000. "A Political Explanation of the Gendered Division of Labor in Japan." Pp. 116–128 in *Gender and Global Restructuring,* edited by Marianne H. Marchand and Anne Sisson Runyan. London: Routledge.

Milligan, Melinda J. 2003. "Displacement and Identity Discontinuity: The Role of Nostalgia in Establishing New Identity Categories." *Symbolic Interaction* 26:381–403.

Morrison, Ann M., Randall P. White, and Ellen Van Velsor. 1987. "The Narrow Band." *Issues and Observations.* Center for Creative Leadership.

———. 1994. *Breaking the Glass Ceiling: Can Women Reach the Top of America's Largest Corporations?* New York: Perseus Press.

Nagase, Nobuko. 2003. "Standard and Nonstandard Work Arrangements, Pay Difference, and Choice of Work by Japanese Mothers." Pp. 267–300 in *Nonstandard Work in Developed Economies: Causes and Consequences,* edited by S. N. Houseman. Kalamazoo, MI: W. E. Upjohn Institute for Employment Research. http://site.ebrary.com/lib/uvalib/Doc?id=10103864.

Nakane, Chie. 1970. *Japanese Society.* Berkeley: University of California Press.

Nevins, Thomas J. 1988. "People Management Is What It's All About." Pp. 127–129 in *Inside the Japanese System,* edited by D. I. Okimoto and T. P. Rohlen. Stanford, CA: Stanford University Press.

Noguchi, Paul H. 1990. *Delayed Departures, Overdue Arrivals: Industrial Familialism and the Japanese National Railways.* Honolulu: University of Hawaii Press.

O'Donnell, Carol. 1984. *The Basis of the Bargain*. Sydney: George Allen and Unwin.

Odaka, Kunio. 1986. *Japanese Management: A Forward-looking Analysis*. Tokyo: Asian Productivity Organization.

Ogasawara, Yuko. 1998. *Office Ladies and Salaried Men: Power, Gender, and Work in Japanese Companies*. Berkeley: University of California Press.

Olthuis, James H. 2000. "Exclusions and Inclusions: Dilemmas of Difference." Pp. 1–10 in *Towards an Ethics of Community: Negotiations of Difference in a Pluralist Society*, edited by James H. Olthuis. Canadian Corporation for Studies in Religion.

Ootsubo, Masako. 1998. "Kintō hō ikkisei wa ima." *Shuukan Diamondo*, April 4, 32–34.

Oskamp, Stuart, and Mark Constanzo (Eds.). 1993. *Gender Issues in Contemporary Society*. London: Sage Publications.

Parreñas, Rhacel Salazar. 2001. *Servants of Globalization: Women, Migration, and Domestic Work*. Stanford: Stanford University Press

Peak, Lois. 1991. *Learning to Go to School in Japan*. Berkeley: University of California Press.

Phelps, Edmund S. 1972. "The Statistical Theory of Racism and Sexism." *American Economic Review* 62:659–661.

Plath, David W. (Ed.). 1983. *Work and Lifecourse in Japan*. Albany: State University of New York Press.

Polley, Douglas. 1997. "Turbulence in Organizations: New Metaphors for Organizational Research." *Organization Science* 8:445–457.

Ram, Rati. 1982. "Sex Differences in the Labor Market Outcomes of Education." Pp. 203–227 in *Women's Education in the Third World: Comparative Perspectives*, edited by G. P. Kelly and C. M. Elliott. Albany: State University of New York Press.

Ramsay, Karen, and Martin Parker. 1992. "Gender, Bureaucracy and Organizational Culture." Pp. 253–276 in *Gender and Bureaucracy*, edited by M. Savage and A. Witz. Oxford, U.K.: Blackwell/ Sociological Review.

Renzetti, Claire M., and Daniel J. Curran. 1989. *Women, Men, and Society: The Sociology of Gender*. Boston: Allyn and Bacon.

Reskin, Barbara F., and Irene Padavic. 1994. *Women and Men at Work*. Thousand Oaks, CA: Pine Forge Press.

Reuther, Cindy, and Gail T. Fairhurst. 2000. "Chaos Theory and the Glass Ceiling." Pp. 236–253 in *Rethinking Organizational and Managerial Communication from Feminist Perspectives*, edited by Patrice M. Buzzanell. Thousand Oaks, CA: Sage Publications.

Ridgeway, Cecilia L. 2001. "Gender, Status, and Leadership." *Journal of Social Issues* 57:637–655.

Robinson, Richard D., John P. Dickson, and John A. Knutsen. 2007. "From Multinational to Transnational?" *International Executive* 35:477–496.

Rohlen, Thomas P. 1974. *For Harmony and Strength: Japanese White-Collar Organization in Anthropological Perspective.* Berkeley: University of California Press.

———. 1975. "The Company Work Group." Pp. 185–209 in *Modern Japanese Organization and Decision-making*, edited by E. F. Vogel. Berkeley: University of California Press.

———. 1979. " 'Permanent Employment' Faces Recession, Slow Growth, and an Aging Work Force." *Journal of Japanese Studies* 5:235–272.

———. 1989. "Order in Japanese Society: Attachment, Authority, and Routine." *Journal of Japanese Studies* 15:5–40.

Sadker, Myra, and David Sadker. 1994. *Failing at Fairness.* New York: Scribner's.

Sakata, Kiriko. 2007. "Gender and Leadership Effectiveness in the Workplace." Pp. 58–83 in *Gender and Career in Japan*, edited by Atsuko Suzuki. Melbourne: Trans Pacific Press.

Samovar, Larry A., and Richard E. Porter. 1999. *Intercultural Communication: A Reader.* Stamford, CT: Wadsworth Publishing.

Sasaki, Masamichi. 2004. "Globalization and National Identity in Japan." *International Journal of Japanese Sociology* 13:69–87.

Saso, Mary. 1990. *Women in the Japanese Workplace.* London: Hilary Shipman.

Savage, Mike. 1992. "Women's Expertise, Men's Authority: Gendered Organization and the Contemporary Middle Classes." Pp. 124–151 in *Gender and Bureaucracy*, edited by M. Savage and A. Witz. Oxford, U.K.: Blackwell/Sociological Review.

Schein, Virginia E. 2001. "A Global Look at Psychological Barriers to Women's Progress in Management." *Journal of Social Issues* 57:675–688.

Schroedel, Jean Reith. 1985. *Alone in a Crowd: Women in the Trades Tell Their Stories.* Philadelphia: Temple University Press.

Segura, Denise A. 1992. "Chicanas in White-Collar Jobs: 'You Have to Prove Yourself More'." *Sociological Perspectives* 35:163–182.

Shibamoto, Janet S. 1985. *Japanese Women's Language.* Orlando, FL: Academic Press.

Shils, Edward. 1994. "Deference." Pp. 197–203 in *Social Stratification: Class, Race, and Gender in Sociological Perspective*, edited by D. B. Grusky. Boulder, CO: Westview Press.

Shuukan Diamondo 1998. "Zadankai: Josei o ikasenai kaisha wa groobaru kyoosoo kara datsuraku suru." April 4, 28.

Skinner, Kenneth. 1983. "Aborted Careers in a Public Corporation." Pp. 50–73 in *Work and Lifecourse in Japan*, edited by D. W. Plath. Albany: State University of New York Press.

Smith, Janet S. 1992. "Women in Charge: Politeness and Directives in the Speech of Japanese Women." *Language in Society* 21:59–82.

Sorenson, Bjorg Aase. 1984. "The Organizational Woman and the Trojan Horse Effect." Pp. 88–105 in *Patriarchy in a Welfare Society*, edited by H. Holter. Oslo: Universitetsforlaget.

Steinhoff, Patricia G., and Kazuko Tanaka. 1993. "Women Managers in Japan." *International Studies of Management and Organization* 23:25–48.

Stevenson, Michael R. 1994. *Gender Roles through the Life Span: A Multidisciplinary Perspective*. Muncie, IN: Ball State University Press.

Strober, Myra H. 1990. "Human Capital Theory: Implications for Human Resources Managers." *Industrial Relations*:214–239.

Strober, Myra H., and Agnes Miling Kaneko Chan. 1999. *The Road Winds Uphill All the Way: Gender, Work, and Family in the United States and Japan*. Cambridge, MA: MIT Press.

Sugimoto, Yoshio. 1997. *An Introduction to Japanese Society*. Cambridge: Cambridge University Press.

Takahashi, Hiroyuki. 1998. "Working Women in Japan: A Look at Historical Trends and Legal Reform." No. 42:1–10. Washington, DC: Japan Economic Institute.

Tanaka, Kazuko. 1995. "Work, Education, and the Family." Pp. 295–308 in *Japanese Women: New Feminist Perspectives on the Past, Present, and Future*, edited by K. Fujimura-Fanselow and A. Kameda. New York: Feminist Press, City University of New York.

Tanaka, Keiko. 1998. "Japanese Women's Magazines: The Language of Aspiration." Pp. 110–132 in *The Worlds of Japanese Popular Culture: Gender, Shifting Boundaries, and Global Culture*, edited by D. P. Martinez. Cambridge: Cambridge University Press.

Tedlock, Dennis. 1979. "The Analogical Tradition and the Emergence of a Dialogical Anthropology." *Journal of Anthropological Research* 35:387–400.

Thiétart, R. A., and B. Forgues. 1995. "Chaos Theory and Organization." *Organization Science* 6:19–31.

Thomas, Landon Jr. 2007. "A Fragile Foothold: The Ranks of Top-Tier Women on Wall St. Are Shrinking," *New York Times*, December 1, B1–B2.

Thompson, James D. 1967. *Organizations in Action*. New York: McGraw-Hill.

Thorne, Barrie. 1993. *Gender Play: Girls and Boys at School*. New Brunswick, NJ: Rutgers University Press.

Time. 2007. "In Japan, A Revolution over Childbearing." February 5.

Tomita, Teruhiko. 1991. "The Intra-organisational Transferability of Japanese-style Management." Pp. 121–146 in *International Business and the Management of Change*, edited by M. Trevor. Aldershot, U.K.: Avebury.

Treiman, Donald J. 1977. *Occupational Prestige in Comparative Perspective.* New York: Academic Press.

Trethewey, Angela. 2000. "Revisioning Control: A Feminist Critique of Disciplined Bodies." Pp. 107–127 in *Rethinking Organizational and Managerial Communication From Feminist Perspectives,* edited by Patrice M. Buzzanell. Thousand Oaks, CA: Sage Publications.

Ueno, Chizuko. 1994. "Women and the Family in Transition in Postindustrial Japan." Pp. 23–42 in *Women of Japan and Korea: Continuity and Change,* edited by J. Gelb and M. L. Palley. Philadelphia: Temple University Press.

Uno, Kathleen S. 1993. "The Death of 'Good Wife, Wise Mother'?" Pp. 293–322 in *Postwar Japan as History,* edited by Andrew Gordon. Berkeley: University of California Press.

Useem, Michael. 1984. *The Inner Circle: Large Corporations and the Rise of Business Political Activity in the U.S. and U.K.* New York: Oxford University Press.

Valian, Virginia. 1999. *Why So Slow? The Advancement of Women.* Cambridge, MA: MIT Press.

Wakabayashi, Mitsuru, and George B. Graen. 1991. "Cross-cultural Human Resource Development: Japanese Manufacturing Firms in Central Japan and Central U.S. States." Pp. 147–172 in *International Business and the Management of Change,* edited by M. Trevor. Aldershot, U.K.: Avebury.

Waller, Marguerite, and Sylvia Marcos (Eds.). 2005. *Dialogue and Difference: Feminisms Challenge Globalization.* New York: Palgrave Macmillan.

Webb, S. 1984. "Gender and Authority in the Workplace." *Studies in Sexual Politics* 1:85–108.

Weber, Max. [1968] 1978. *Economy and Society.* Berkeley: University of California Press.

Wesselius, Janet Catherina. 2000. "'Woman' in the Plural: Negotiating Sameness and Difference in Feminist Theory." Pp. 74–90 in *Towards an Ethics of Community: Negotiations of Difference in a Pluralist Society,* edited by James H. Olthuis. Canadian Corporation for Studies in Religion.

West, Candace, and Don H. Zimmerman. 1991. "Doing Gender." Pp. 13–37 in *The Social Construction of Gender,* edited by J. Lorber and S. Farrell. Newbury Park, CA: Sage Publications.

White, Merry. 1987. *The Japanese Educational Challenge: A Commitment to Children.* New York: Free Press.

———. 1993. *The Material Child: Coming of Age in Japan and America.* Berkeley: University of California Press.

Williams, Joan. 2000. *Unbending Gender: Why Family and Work Conflict and What to Do about It.* New York: Oxford University Press.

Witz, Anne, and Mike Savage. 1992. "The Gender of Organizations." Pp. 3–62 in *Gender and Bureaucracy*, edited by M. Savage and A. Witz. Oxford, U.K.: Blackwell/ Sociological Review.

Wright, Erik Olin, Janeen Baxter, and Gunn Elisabeth Birkelund. 1995. "The Gender Gap in Workplace Authority: A Cross-National Study." *American Sociological Review* 60:407–435.

Zimmeck, Meta. 1992. "Marry in Haste, Repent at Leisure: Women, Bureaucracy and the Post Office, 1870–1920." Pp. 65–93 in *Gender and Bureaucracy*, edited by M. Savage and A. Witz. Oxford, U.K.: Blackwell/ Sociological Review.

 Index

Ellen V. Fuller is Assistant Professor of East Asian Languages, Literatures and Cultures and Studies in Women and Gender at the University of Virginia.